LET'S TALK ABOUT

TRUTH

"Once again, Ann Garrido offers a thoughtful and practical contribution to thinking about ministry. In *Let's Talk about Truth*, she cautions ministers against using truth as a cudgel and instead shows us how to speak authentically about truth in ways that those who hear us will understand. I happily recommend this book to leaders of the Church at every level."

Rev. Gerard Olinger, C.S.C.
Vice President for Mission Engagement and Church Affairs
University of Notre Dame

"With wit and wisdom, Ann Garrido provides a master class in explaining not only how we can address the surprisingly contentious topic of truth as Catholic leaders but also why now, more than ever, we must do so with passion, clarity, conviction, and care. *Let's Talk about Truth* is a brilliant look at why the words we say—including those we type on screens and blast out into cyberspace—must give witness to the Church's understanding of truth as a way of life as well as our ultimate end. Garrido makes our work lighter, and I will certainly draw on her wisdom as I prepare talks, write articles, and engage social media."

Katie Prejean McGrady
Author of *Follow* and *Room 24*

"As a veteran Catholic educator, I aim always to respond to student questions in truth yet with both clarity and charity. During this era of deep division both inside and outside of the Church, Ann Garrido provides anyone of good will with the encouragement and tools needed to profess the goodness, truth, and beauty of the Good News of Jesus Christ in all that we do."

Justin McClain
Theology teacher at Bishop McNamara High School
Forestville, Maryland

"Ann Garrido has done it again: taken an old topic that might seem abstract or well-worn and injected it with new life. Garrido takes the reader on an adventure which shows us that 'truth' contains some exciting inner dynamics for the preacher and hearer to explore together. In our post-truth milieu, this is a timely, needed, and fresh approach to a mainstay of Christian faith."

Rev. Michael Connors, C.S.C.
Director of the John S. Marten Program in Homiletics and Liturgics
University of Notre Dame

"An essential read for any minister who is trying to reclaim truth as a fundamental human and explicitly Christian value. Amid tweets and talking heads, Ann Garrido inspires us to discern and live the truth. She challenges preachers, teachers, and other Christian leaders to see the world as it is, seek a sound basis for judgments, speak honestly, and be faithful in relationships."

Theresa Rickard, O.P.
President of RENEW International

"I have witnessed firsthand the denial of truth, of reality, of what *actually* is, mostly on social media. I have heard the voices that do not believe in truth—any truth. We who have the mission to preach, teach, and lead must confront our post-truth culture directly and help others to do so in their everyday lives. I applaud Ann Garrido's work in *Let's Talk about Truth*. She masterfully speaks to the truth of things within the mystery of creation and Creator."

Most Rev. David P. Talley
Bishop of Memphis

"Ann Garrido, a remarkably entrepreneurial theologian, writes of truth as seeing the world, forming good judgments, communicating with others, and being in relationship. In four concise chapters, she shows us what each looks like in the particularities of preaching, teaching, and other types of Church leadership. Garrido dares to look truth in the face and to preach about it!"

Rev. Gregory Heille, O.P.
Professor of Preaching and Evangelization
Director, Doctor of Ministry in Preaching
Aquinas Institute of Theology

LET'S TALK ABOUT

TRUTH

A Guide for Preachers, Teachers, and Other Catholic Leaders in a World of Doubt and Discord

ANN M. GARRIDO

AVE MARIA PRESS AVE Notre Dame, Indiana

© 2020 by Ann M. Garrido

Founded in 1865, Ave Maria Press is a ministry of the United States Province of Holy Cross.

www.avemariapress.com

Paperback: ISBN-13 978-1-59471-961-5

E-book: ISBN-13 978-1-59471-962-2

Cover image © Pietro Rolandi/Eye Em/Getty Images.

Cover and text design by Samantha Watson.

Printed and bound in the United States of America.

Library of Congress Cataloging-in-Publication Data is available.

To Micah,
who radiates truth in his deeds.

This truth is not spoken so much with a speech.
It is a way of being, a way of living
and you see it in every single deed.
—Pope Francis
General Audience
November 14, 2018

CONTENTS

INTRODUCTION

Now admit it. You almost didn't pick up this book because it has "truth" in its title, and who wants to talk about truth nowadays? According to who you ask, it has become too noxious to talk about, too wearying to talk about, too heated to talk about, or too impossible to talk about. Mention the word from the pulpit and people tune out . . . or write letters to your bishop. They accuse you of being too political . . . or too out of touch with the world today. The word has become tarnished—mottled and blackened with misuse and misunderstanding. So, can we who preach, teach, and lead in a broken Church floundering in a tangled culture still talk about truth?

Grammarians will suggest I have the question wrong. Shouldn't it be "May we talk about truth?" But that's easy. Of course, preachers, teachers, and others who lead *may* talk about truth. Depending on your favored translation, the word *truth* appears in the Bible over two hundred times. It is a frequent theme in the writings of recent popes and consistently weaves its way through stories of the saints. We might even say that it is such a central theme in Christianity that it is the *duty* of preachers and others who lead to talk about truth.

But there are so many ways it can go wrong, and has. When I started floating drafts of this project among friends, one immediately wrote back, "Truth is a trigger word for me, having been beaten up by it in the past. . . . [I] get anxious when someone

1

wants to preach on truth. . . . [It was] used as a club over my head."[1] Not an uncommon reaction. Sincere and good-willed religious leaders, impelled by a sense of preaching duty, sometimes end up doing harm, turning people off not only to the truth of Jesus Christ but to the very notion of truth itself. As a preaching instructor, I have watched any number of preaching students go about their initial attempts with gusto—the word *truth* sprinkled in every other sentence that comes out of their mouths—while the opening chords of "Fools Rush In" play in the back of my head. We *may* talk about truth, but I'm not sure it is having the impact we want.

At the same time, I suspect the experienced preaching angels who no longer dare to tread in the vocabulary of truth are not doing us any favors either. Aware of the dangers and complexity of the term, many back away from talking about truth in the pulpit altogether, unintentionally contributing to the profound cultural confusion we now find ourselves in—what many have termed a *post-truth society*. These preachers and their counterparts in teaching and pastoral leadership cede their duty to address the topic and, as a result, many Christians' ongoing instruction on truth has come only in the form of debating heads and Facebook memes. We live in hope that giving differing perspectives equal airtime will somehow lead to greater clarity and consensus on issues, but lost in the conversation is something fundamental: Does it matter whether these varying perspectives offered are true? In our present moment in history, can we still talk about truth?

The question is not "May we?" (Answer: Yes.) And the question is not "Should we?" (Answer: Also yes.) The question is "Can we?" That's harder, because it requires we figure out a way to overcome both our brazen certainty and our untimely reticence in order to speak effectively on a contentious concept with equally certain and reticent hearers. It's harder because these are hearers who've tried and so often failed in their own conversations about truth with families and friends. It's harder because they come to us angry, tired, and belittled. They come to us—like my friend—triggered and wounded. It's harder because their experiences have left them wrestling with a whole skein of tangled questions: "What is truth? Why does it even matter? Does anyone really know what's true? Who's to judge? Aren't we all entitled to our own opinions? What am I supposed to do when others don't agree with what I know is true? What do I do if someone is lying? Isn't it best to sometimes fudge the truth? Why can't we all just get along? How do I stay friends with someone who's so clearly wrong? Should I even bother to host Thanksgiving dinner again?"

Can we really disentangle *that* knotted mess? Given the current climate, can we still say something meaningful about truth from the pulpit—and by extension in the classroom and in the board-room—that could help real hearers in real time?

Yes, I think we can.

What gives me hope is my own story. Granted, I might have a bit more of an obsession with questions of truth than most. My mom traces my fixation to the Santa Claus Incident of 1976. Apparently, when I found out that Santa Claus wasn't real, I "didn't handle the news very well." That is her description, not mine. I say I "handled the news" as any perfectly reasonable person would upon discovering the world wasn't the place she had imagined it to be and that she had been lied to on this matter for her entire life by parents, aunts, uncles, older cousins, and the much-treasured J. C. Penney's Christmas catalog.

My high school journals are peppered with statements such as "Then he said . . . but the truth of the matter is . . ." and "Honestly, I don't think it's fair that . . ." As a teenager, I was pretty sure I had a handle on the truth. I knew things. I didn't doubt myself. I doubted my parents. But I didn't doubt my own ability to assess how things "really are."

Time in Africa as a college student turned that confidence upside down and shook it like a cocktail. Teaching for four years on the island of Guam shook my assumptions even more. The experience of being married and having a child dropped a cherry on top. I had thought I knew what was real, but clearly I had been wrong. Who's right? Can anyone know anything for certain? How can two people of goodwill who love each other still see things so differently?

What kept me tethered on this tumultuous ride was my ongoing relationship with the wider Church community. I was blessed throughout my childhood, my teen years, my college campus ministry years, and then into my adult years with a handful of extraordinary preachers and teachers who helped me work through my questions and disappointments (of which the Santa Claus Incident was but the first). They did so by drawing on the rich Catholic tradition surrounding the topic of truth, and it made a world of difference to me. They helped me understand that I wasn't the first one to be asking these questions or suffering these disappointments. I wasn't the only one to wonder about how we know what we know or the best way to build a life in a world filled with ambiguity. Slowly and surely, they disentangled my own knot of questions and assumptions and, when they couldn't sort the knot themselves, they taught me how to stay with the knot and not give up.

Among my most treasured interlocutors have been members of the Order of Preachers, more widely known as the Dominican Order. The Dominicans were founded with a charism for truth—a special tenacity in pursuing truth-related questions when others would have called it a day. They offered me a doorway into the theology of truth, or to use Anselm of Canterbury's classic definition, faith seeking an *understanding* of truth. They introduced me to Thomas Aquinas, who thought and wrote about this topic more than most in human history. But after twenty years, I would say the Dominicans' greatest gift has been introducing me to a *spirituality* of truth, which I am going to define as "faith seeking a way to *live* truth." I root this definition in Jesus' conversation with Nicodemus, found in the Gospel of John. Jesus tells his nighttime disciple that only the one who *"lives* the truth comes to the light"

(Jn 3:21). In the same way that "live the bicycle" sounds to me like another way to describe "bicycling," "live the truth" sounds to me as if Jesus thinks of truth more as a verb than a noun. He wants us to engage in the act of "truthing." The Dominicans are adamant that truth is meant to be understood as a whole way of life, and by the witness of *their* lives have given me some idea of how that works.

The Dominicans were also founded with a charism for preaching—a special tenacity for keeping a conversation going even when the issues at stake are hard to articulate and nuance is of the essence. It has been an honor over the course of the past two decades to become ever more enfolded into their preaching mission and to be invited to think together with them about how we might articulate and nuance truthing better. They also know there are so many ways it can go wrong. In eight centuries, they've had the chance to mess up a time or two . . . or two thousand. My point here is simply that preaching about truth is tricky, teaching about truth is tricky, leading others in pursuit of truth is tricky—not only at this moment in time but in every age of history. Dominicans have taught me that we need not get discouraged by our failures and abandon talking about truth, but rather learn from our messes and continue to sort what works from what doesn't.

WHAT DO WE WANT TO SAY?

So, if we wanted to take on the challenge of talking about truth in a positive, impactful way (no clubs over the head!), what is the wisdom of the broader Catholic tradition—rooted in scripture and reflected upon by the Church for twenty centuries—that we want hearers to access and *live* related to truth? Where do we even begin?

First, a word about where we won't begin: In this book, you will find little discussion of God as Truth or Jesus as Truth, or the Bible and Catholic doctrine as Truth—capital-*T* Truth. Like you, I share the conviction that all these are Truth. But we cannot begin there because such statements presume we (including our hearers) all share a common understanding of what the word *truth* means, and I do not think we can presume that anymore, dare I say even among devout Catholics. Those who see their ministry as "preaching the Truth" often begin with an unnecessarily narrow definition of small-*t* truth. Capitalizing the *T* does not expand their definition; it only means that we begin to look at God, Jesus, the Bible, and doctrine in correspondingly narrow ways.

The situation mirrors trying to preach "God is Love" in a congregation riddled with domestic violence or sexual abuse. If these are the experiences that have shaped members' definition of love, then applying the term *love* to God in this context is more harmful than helpful. We would need to remedy the hearers' definition of love first—clarifying what love is not and widening their understanding of what love is.

We will return to Truth at the end of the book. But first we need to take a step back. We need to start by clarifying for ourselves and for our hearers what small-*t* truth is not and widening our understanding of what small-*t* truth is. Indeed, we want to do a 360 view of the term. Doing a 360 requires we position ourselves to look at truth from a number of directions. Like the mysterious cherubim in the biblical book of Ezekiel, we could say that truth—as pondered in the broader Catholic tradition—has four faces, each concerning itself with a different aspect of our human struggle and each speaking to a different set of our oh-so-difficult questions. Or using the metaphor of a diamond, perhaps it is easier to visualize truth as having four facets.

1. *One facet of truth gazes upon our lifelong struggle to perceive the world as accurately as possible.* It concerns itself with making sure that our minds are aligned with what really is, rather than imaginary things. It recognizes that a solid picture of reality is essential for

our survival, so it cares a great deal about our ability to grasp *the facts*.

2. *A second facet of truth watches over our struggle to interpret the happenings of our world and make sense of them.* Recognizing that we live in a pluralistic society that interprets things in many different ways, it is concerned with our ability to judge among various interpretations and opinions to fashion lives that are oriented toward *the good*.

3. *A third facet of truth focuses on our struggle to communicate with one another toward the building up of society.* Because society depends on being able to trust one another's words, it is concerned with our human propensities to lie or share half-truths as well as our propensity to say too much. It wants to help us find the right balance, or what we might call *the truthful*, in our speech.

4. *A fourth facet of truth considers our struggle to "be true" in long-term relationships with one another.* It is concerned with our capacity to remain faithful in the kinds of ways that God is faithful, even in times of profound disagreement with one another. It wants to help us figure out which actions are the *most loving*.

Each of these facets has something distinctive to contribute toward our efforts at living truth in a post-truth world. At the same time, no single facet of truth can stand alone. Each facet needs the other three to fully represent the tradition's wisdom on truth. As we begin to look for opportunities to talk about truth from the pulpit, in the classroom, and in the boardroom over the course of the liturgical year, we want to look for opportunities to introduce and reflect upon all the varied facets of truth, rather than speaking repeatedly of only one facet of the whole.

THE ART OF PUBLIC SPEAKING

As Catholic preachers, teachers, and other Church leaders, talking about truth effectively requires not only knowing the tradition's

wisdom on the matter but also knowing how to share it in a way
that can be understood and remembered. Because I am a teacher
of homiletics, I will write much of what I want to communicate
in this book from the perspective of preaching, leaving to you, at
least at times, the imaginative connections to other kinds of leading
and talking about truth in the life of the Church.

We all know very well-educated preachers who lose their congregations during their opening lines. Likewise, we've watched
teachers losing the class, or bishops, pastors, directors of religious
education, and other ministry team leaders losing their audiences
early and irredeemably. Why is this? Let's consider what we are
learning about preaching from the field of homiletics about what
doesn't work that can inform all of our public speaking in the
Church.

- *Preaching that has multiple points doesn't work.* For a good portion
  of the Church's history, preaching was a form of evening
  entertainment in the community, and before the advent of
  widespread literacy, hearers were capable of listening for long
  periods of time and holding multiple thoughts. Literacy, and
  now the advent of visual media, has changed the way people hear. The modern mind cannot absorb by ear what the
  ancients did.
- *Preaching that uses lots of academic (including theological) language
  doesn't work.* Preachers should be steeped in theology but able
  to communicate theology in an accessible manner. Academic
  language works in writing because it allows the writer to con-
  dense a great deal of information into a small space, but it does
  not register in the ear of most of the faithful. Words that have
  Latin prefixes and suffixes do not stick in hearers' memories.
- *Preaching that is disconnected from hearers' lives doesn't work.* Hearers
  tune out when preachers attempt to answer questions they
  personally are not asking and offer examples that feel distant
  from their everyday realities.

- *Preaching that robs hearers of their moral freedom doesn't work.* Hearers do not like to be told what to do or have their current efforts to live their faith underappreciated by the preacher. Multiple *shoulds*, *musts*, and *need tos* make hearers tune out.
- *Preaching that sets up an us-versus-them mentality doesn't work.* Preaching that condemns or demonizes a particular group or viewpoint increases the engagement of hearers who already share the preacher's perspective, but for hearers who in any way empathize with the *them*, it increases the likelihood of dismissing the entirety of what the preacher has to say, not only in the preaching at hand but in future preaching as well.

What are we learning about preaching that works best?

- *Preaching that works has one point.* The preacher can use multiple examples and experiment with creative forms to get that one point across, but afterward listeners should be able to summarize the preacher's key message in thirty words or less. You know that a preacher has reached a basic level of effectiveness if various hearers can summarize the preacher's key message in much the same way.
- *Preaching that works imitates conversational language.* Even if a preacher chooses to write out a text, the language used needs to imitate how people talk in everyday speech. Pope Francis calls for preaching in the kind of language a mother uses when talking to her children. I imagine the speech patterns of friends who've had one beer or glass of wine together. The most effective language evokes the senses so that the message registers not just in the hearers' minds but also in their bodies.
- *Preaching that works is strangely specific.* Hearers want to sense that the preacher knows and loves them. They perk up when the preacher speaks to a question that they personally have been wrestling with and relates stories that mirror the dynamics of their own experiences, even if the details are quite different.

Curiously, generic preaching examples (e.g., "We all have experienced going to the grocery store . . .") register far less than highly specific references (e.g., "I was musing in the cereal aisle . . ."). The latter sticks in the mind even if the hearer doesn't eat cereal.

- *Preaching that works emphasizes autonomy and appreciation.* Effective preaching presumes goodwill on the part of hearers and highlights the efforts they are already making to live the Gospel. It also acknowledges their freedom to respond or not to the preacher's message, realizing that the hearers will need to be the ones who decide how to embed the message in their particular lives.

- *Preaching that works anticipates a diversity of perspectives.* Effective preaching acknowledges a diversity of viewpoints and assumes that diversity is present within any group of hearers. The preacher treats viewpoints different from their own with the greatest charity possible, conveying a sense that "we're all trying to figure this out together."

Why have I stopped at five bullets in each category? Because five is the maximum that even readers can absorb at any one time. But also because I think these five bullets capture the basics we want to hold to as we attempt to preach on any topic, including the topic of truth.

How Will This Book Help You Talk about Truth?

Our job as preachers, teachers, and Church leaders is to marry the wide wisdom of the tradition regarding truth with the marks of effective preaching and see what kinds of sparks fly. Maybe we can help ancient ideas feel relevant again. Maybe we will be able to clarify for hearers what now seems so befuddled. Maybe we can recover a space for truth in everyday conversation. Maybe we can offer powerful witness as to what it means to live truth in our post-truth era. Are you getting excited about exploring these possibilities with me? Feeling a little less weary than when you picked up this book and a little more curious about what you might try in your own community?

In this book I've taken the liberty to sort the messy everyday truth questions raised earlier into four categories, corresponding to the four facets of truth. (I've added a few more that your hearers probably aren't currently asking but likely will once you open Pandora's box on the topic of truth, because I want you to feel prepared.) Each chapter summarizes a bit of wisdom from the Catholic tradition to help contemporary hearers wrestle with their questions—certainly not all that could be said on the topic, but a place to begin. Even if we can't resolve these questions once and for all, we'll discover that tradition gives us frames for thinking and talking about truth that can ease the consternation so many of us are feeling at present and inspire ideas for moving forward. (One question I will not address is what to do about hosting Thanksgiving dinner. I think even Thomas Aquinas would back away from that one!)

Sample preaching texts are integrated throughout each chapter to illumine how you might share tradition's insights from the pulpit while trying to hold to the markers of effective preaching I've described. Most of the preaching samples included have been shared in congregations during the past few years. In some cases, the text has been revised significantly based on congregational response. The samples represent preaching I have done in a variety of settings—Eucharist, Liturgy of the Hours, retreats, online reflections, workshop openings. (So many opportunities we have to talk about truth and to invite others to talk about truth!) The danger in offering any preaching text is that an event meant to be aural is experienced instead in writing, and the connection to a very specific group of hearers is lost. But my hope is that in reviewing tested samples, you become increasingly confident that you also *may*, *should*, and—most importantly—*can* talk about truth from the pulpit, in your classroom, or at the board table. By the end of the book I want what presently feels daunting to feel more manageable. I want you to close the back cover and say to yourself, "No doubt about it, I can do this!"

Before you close that cover, I've included a preaching assessment tool that you can use when reviewing the preaching samples, checking them against the marks of effective preaching I've described. I won't be offended if you don't think every preaching hits every mark. Maybe you will want to take a stab at editing some of these samples to make them more effective. You might want to make copies of this assessment to review your own preaching texts, lecture notes, or pastoral announcements as well. Because truth is such a multifaceted topic, and it is so challenging to preach, teach, or simply talk about truth effectively, if you are regularly engaged in these ministries of the Word, consider inviting others who do likewise to share their own preaching texts, lessons, lectures, or videos to review together. We can continue to learn about how best to talk about truth from one another's successes, and perhaps even more from one another's flops. Questions for personal reflection and/or dialogue within small groups have been included at the end of each chapter.

There are many days I turn on the television and still "do not handle the news well." But increasingly there are days when I think as a preacher and teacher I can be a part of the solution. I can be part of retrieving that tarnished word *truth* from the world of debating heads and conflicting memes, and with some spit and hard work, help truth recover a bit of its luster. I *can* talk about truth in positive, impactful ways. And, best of all, I can be a part of living truth in this present age, sure of the coming light.

A preaching sample to get us started . . .

Preaching Sample:
LIVING THE TRUTH
SCRIPTURE TEXT:
JOHN 3:19–21

> And this is the verdict, that the light came into the world, but people preferred darkness to light, because their works were evil. For everyone who does wicked things hates the light and does not come toward the light, so that his works might not be exposed. But whoever lives the truth comes to the light, so that his works may be clearly seen as done in God.

Your roommates both insist that the traffic ticket in today's mail must be yours because they don't run yellow lights—ever. Never mind that you were camping in another state the date the ticket was issued and had left them with the car keys.

You sit and watch as your boss regales potential investors with glowing predictions regarding the industry's future. Big growth right around the corner. Just as she's predicted for the past decade . . . except now she's absolutely sure of it.

Your uncle monopolizes Thanksgiving dinner arguing that Earth is flat.

The politician on the nightly news swears that he had no idea his staff was engaged in underhanded activities. In the weather segment that follows, the meteorologist forecasts the coming week's weather using every apocalyptic reference found in the Bible.

Your friend is sure that her fiancé will cut down on his drinking after they are married. She's not sure that she believes in God. All that "opium of the masses" stuff. But she believes in her fiancé because he's promised he'll stop. And the seventeenth time is a charm. Don't worry, she says, it's gonna be fine.

But it's not fine. It's not fine at all, because Earth is *not* flat and that is *not* your traffic ticket. Your friend is fooling herself. The politician is lying. Next week's rain will *not* surpass Noah's deluge, and your boss must be pulling her numbers straight from the bingo ball spinner over in the church hall. Is no one in contact with reality? Doesn't anyone care anymore about—go ahead and say it—truth? Because that's what's in question in each of these scenarios, isn't it? Truth. And you care about it.

According to Jewish lore, when God formed the first human from the clay of the earth, God breathed life into the creature and roused it into action by way of exhaling a single Hebrew word—*emet*—in English, "truth." And to this very day, if you want to start another's heart beating and blood pulsing and mind racing, just broach the topic: What is truth? How do you know such and such is true? Are you telling the truth here? *Truth* is a word that still puts fire in human bones.

It certainly seems to have put a lot of fire in Jesus' bones. The gospels record Jesus speaking of truth nineteen times. Even his naysayers regarded him as someone who cares about truth (Lk 20:21). Indeed, Jesus appears to have had a distinctive speech pattern, found nowhere else in literature, in which he begins many of his teachings with the interjection "Amen!" or even "Amen! Amen!" This word *Amen*—closely related to the Hebrew word *emet* (and sometimes translated "Truly!" in English)—appears at the start of one of Jesus' sentences no fewer than seventy-five times in the Bible.

When Jesus speaks of truth, though, he doesn't use the word as we often use it now; he doesn't talk of truth as something he "has." Mysteriously, he claims truth is something he "is" (Jn 14:6). Indeed, he often speaks of truth as if it is bigger than him—something he "testifies to" (Jn 18:37); something we are invited to "belong to" (Jn 18:37) or "worship in" (Jn 4:24). Most intriguingly, in today's passage from the Gospel of John, he speaks of truth almost as a verb. Depending on the translation, Jesus says that truth is something that we must "live," "practice," or "do" if we want to "come to the light." But what does it mean to "live truth"?

You are not the first person to ask the question. Many of Jesus' followers have wondered the same and spent their lives scouring the scriptures and reading the great philosophers looking for clues. While I can't tell you how to win the argument with your crazy uncle, I can—and do—invite you today to join in the age-old quest to become a person who lives truth. *How?*

First, in how you see. Classical Christianity describes truth as having a picture of the world in your mind that corresponds to the world as it actually is. For example: It is true that the chair I am about to sit upon really does exist. It is true that the earth orbits the sun in a 365.25-day cycle. It is true I weigh 141 pounds today. It's important that we get that kind of stuff right because if I try to sit in a chair that isn't there, I will injure myself. If I suspend myself from a rope that only promises to hold up to 120 pounds, I could kill myself. If I miscalculate the length of a year and plant crops in the wrong season, I will go hungry. At a most fundamental level, living truth means always seeking a more accurate understanding of the world as it really is—not as I wish it to be but as it really is.

Living truth, however, means more than just knowing a bunch of facts about reality. It requires the ability to figure out which facts to pay attention to and how to put those facts together in a way that makes sense so that the world becomes more comprehensible and you can live in it well.

So, a *second way of living truth involves becoming aware of how you arrive at conclusions about things*. For example, we will often say things such as "It is true that my alma mater is an amazing school." "It is true that the death penalty is wrong." "It is true Billy should be punished for his actions." These kinds of statements aren't facts; they are judgments we make—opinions that we form based on facts we have and which ones we consider important. Sometimes you'll hear people say, "Well, everyone is entitled to their own opinion." But what we forget is that everyone is obligated to make sure they are forming their opinions with the best information possible, considering the impact they have on others. Living truth means being willing to explore and assess the worthiness of your opinions.

Third, living truth involves how you talk. It's one thing to have a mind that grasps reality accurately and can build it into a coherent picture. It's another thing to say to others what it is that you've grasped in your mind. Not only do your brain and reality have to line up but your brain and your words have to line up as well. For example: It's true that I gave the project my all only if I really did give it my all. It's true that I'll support lower taxes when I'm elected only if that is what I actually will do. This way of living truth is what is referred to as "truthfulness."

Finally, living truth impacts how you relate to others. We'd be missing something if we ended without returning to our Jewish roots. Remember the Hebrew word for truth—*emet*—that I mentioned earlier? *Emet* means more than accuracy or honesty. At its core, *emet* means faithfulness, reliability, protective strength you can count on. In Bible-speak, the Word of God is *emet*. The judgments of God are *emet*. Truth in this sense is the truth of marriage vows: I promise to be true to you in good times and in bad, in sickness and in health, till death do us part. Living truth means being faithful in our relationships, being someone who others can count on.

Hebrew language scholars are quick to point out that *emet* is but one letter away from *met*, the Hebrew word for "death." We might wonder whether this is purely a quirk of the language or whether it suggests a deeper insight: living truth has a "wholeness" to it. We can't just pick one of these areas to be committed to; we need to embrace the "doing" of truth in all four. It does not help to honestly share our opinions if our opinions aren't grounded in reality. It can be harmful to speak truthfully if we don't have any concern for the people we are speaking to. Things go awry if we pay attention to one aspect of reality but ignore others. If we want to come to "the light" that Jesus talks about, we must be serious about letting the practice of truth permeate every area of our lives, because removing even one letter from the word can put us on a path toward destruction.

Imagine what would happen if each of us in our own homes, workplaces, schools, and neighborhoods committed to these four practices this week:

- seeing things as accurately as possible;
- forming our opinions as carefully as possible;
- speaking as honestly as possible; and
- being as faithful to one another as possible.

What would the world look like? I suspect we would enjoy that "light" Jesus speaks of in today's gospel reading. But even more so, I suspect we would become that "light to the nations" that the Bible speaks about so often—a powerful and attractive witness to our politicians and bosses, family and friends. Maybe even our crazy uncles.

1.

Truth

AS A WAY
OF SEEING
THE WORLD

In the introduction, I named four distinct albeit interrelated angles from which the Catholic tradition reflects on the word *truth*. The first way of understanding the term—the one most familiar to philosophers and scientists—is the classical definition of truth posed by Thomas Aquinas, based on the earlier thinking of the philosopher Aristotle: "*Veritas est adaequatio rei et intellectus.*"[1] Literally translated, "Truth is the adequation of thing and intellect." Or more simply put, truth means having a mental picture in your head that is aligned with reality: You don't want to be seeing things that aren't really there. You *do* want to be able to see accurately the things that *are* there.

WHY DOES IT MATTER?

One of the questions raised in our post-truth society is whether or not seeing things accurately even matters. Ever heard a member of your congregation or a student in your classroom say something such as "It's hard to know what's real and what's not anymore, and yet life goes on. Why should I care?"? The Catholic tradition considers strange this nonchalance regarding matters of truth. On an eminently practical level, it asserts we *should* care because our lives—indeed the life of our planet—depend on it.

In contrast to some Eastern spiritual traditions, Catholicism starts with the premise that there *is* such a thing as reality. The world is not something that just exists in our minds. It exists on its own—whether we are aware of it or not, whether we believe in it or not. The climate is warming or it is not warming, but the existence of global warming is not changed by whether you agree it is warming. God exists or God does not exist, but God's existence does not depend on whether you believe in God. Beliefs do, however, impact our lives. You may not believe in gravity, but if you step out of a fourth-story window, you are just as likely to fall to the ground as the person who does. If in your mind you perceive things other than how they really are, you run into all kinds of problems. Consider the well-worn tale of a radio conversation between a US naval vessel and Canadian authorities one foggy night off the coast of Newfoundland:

> *Americans*: Please divert your course ten degrees to the north to avoid a collision.
> *Canadians*: Recommend you divert *your* course ten degrees to the north to avoid a collision.
> *Americans*: This is the captain of a US Navy ship. I say again, divert ten degrees north.
> *Canadians*: No, I say again: it is urgent you divert *your* course.

Americans: This is the aircraft carrier USS *Missouri*, the second largest ship in the US Atlantic fleet. We are accompanied by three destroyers, two cruisers, and numerous support vessels. I demand that you change your course ten degrees, that's one zero degrees north, or countermeasures will be undertaken to ensure the safety of this ship.

Canadians: This is a lighthouse. Your call.

Reality is what it is. No matter who we are or how powerful we like to think of ourselves as being, we stand in danger of a terrible crash if we have the wrong picture of "what is" in our minds.

Church writings, hence, often refer to truth as "objective"—a way of asserting that our survival and thriving as a species depends on getting as objective a mental picture of reality as possible, unfiltered by illusion, bias, or prejudice. But there is a second—and I would suggest, equally important—way of understanding this claim. When we say truth is "objective," we also are asserting that truth always remains a goal before us. In the same way that a syllabus lists up front the course objectives, truth is something we aspire to. Something that we shoot for—not something we possess. Truth is an ongoing effort. Like justice, humility, or courage, it is something we must practice. With much practice we might get quite good at it. But it is not something we would ever say we've mastered. No one says, "I've got this justice thing under control" or "I'm as humble as one could get." The person brazen enough to say, "I possess courage," appears to the rest of the world as if they are itching (foolishly) to be tested in battle. Lifelong soldiers know better than to make such a claim.

The purely objective nature of truth becomes all the clearer when we consider again what truth is aiming for: an accurate picture of *reality*. That is no small task! Who could ever say, "I've accurately counted the number of stars in the universe," "I've got the mystery of weather all wrapped up," or "I've adequately grasped what makes people tick"? As one of my colleagues is keen to say, "Reality is like a bazillion volts of electricity and most of us are only dealing with 60-watt bulbs." Even if we happen to be lucky enough to possess a 100-watt bulb in our own skull, in the grand scheme of things, the difference is not all that great. So, far from implying that "we've got reality under wraps," Catholicism's insistence on objective truth implies that *we know* there is always more to know, and *we see* that our looking glass could always be more polished, which opens up the possibility that *we could be wrong about some things*. To summarize in the words of the philosopher Michael Lynch, "If I know anything, it is that I don't know everything and neither does anyone else."[2]

While asserting the importance of objective truth, then, as a preacher, teacher, or other leader, you'll want to be especially careful how you use the term. You want to invite people to desire and actively seek a deeper understanding of reality, but you never want to speak about truth as something that they will end up possessing as a result of that quest. Indeed, one of the most significant stumbling blocks to doing truth as a way of life is the belief that one already has it. Aquinas does not define truth as a particular body of content, so much as a way of being in right relationship with a reality much larger than ourselves, a way of practicing holiness in our minds.

In the preaching that follows, I attempt to put hearers back in contact with their own innate desire to see reality as the beginning point for living truth—in other words, to reestablish truth as a primary objective in life. I see such efforts as foundational in trying to rebuild truth as a Christian practice in modern society: if hearers do not first desire to know what is real, doing truth will hold no attraction for them.

Preaching Sample:
DO YOU WANT TO SEE?

THIRTIETH SUNDAY IN ORDINARY TIME YEAR B

SCRIPTURE TEXT: MARK 10:46–52

[A]s he was leaving Jericho with his disciples and a sizable crowd, Bartimaeus, a blind man, the son of Timaeus, sat by the roadside begging. On hearing that it was Jesus of Nazareth, he began to cry out and say, "Jesus, son of David, have pity of me." And many rebuked him, telling him to be silent. But he kept calling out all the more, "Son of David, have pity on me." Jesus stopped and said, "Call him." So they called the blind man, saying to him, "Take courage; get up, he is calling you." He threw aside his cloak, sprang up, and came to Jesus. Jesus said to him in reply, "What do you want me to do for you?" The blind man replied to him, "Master I want to see." Jesus told him, "Go your way; your faith has saved you." Immediately he received his sight and followed him on the way.

I want you to imagine for a moment that there exists a machine that could let you experience whatever you want. Once you are inside this machine, you could live in the virtual reality of your dreams. You could have your grandma's homemade spaghetti and meatballs every night of the week, if you want. With the flick of a switch, the scenery around you could change so that suddenly you could be in an exotic destination such as Maui, Manhattan, or Marrakesh . . . whatever floats your boat. It would allow you to experience what it'd be like to have box seats on the fifty-yard line for all your favorite football team's games. In this machine, you could have long lingering conversations with famous characters from history . . . and the barista would never close up shop.

Now, none of this would be real. It would all be virtual. *But it would feel real.* In fact, we could even arrange it so that once you were inside the machine, you wouldn't even remember that you were only inside a machine. You wouldn't remember ever having any other life outside this dream one. That'd be pretty amazing, eh? But here's the catch: Once you go inside the machine, you can never come out. You have to stay within this virtual life for the remainder of your life. Would you do it?[3] Well, would you?

My guess is that—even as the burgeoning reality industry makes such an option more and more possible—most of us, if we sat with the idea long enough, would say no. There is something wired into the human spirit that wants to be in contact with what is real.

Now, "the real" is not the *only* thing that we want as humans. We have other conflicting desires: the desire to be accepted, the desire to be comfortable, the desire for excitement. And in any given moment, we might favor a temporary virtual illusion that meets one of those other desires rather than staring into reality—which, let's face it, can sometimes be unaccepting, uncomfortable, and unexciting. But, *over the long haul*, given the choice between being loved by a virtual person or being loved by a real person, I think most of us would pick a real person. And, *over the long haul*, we'd rather know what the real person who loves us *really* thinks of us rather than hold a fictitious view of what they think of us. The desire for the real is deeply twisted into our DNA.

That desire lies at the heart of our gospel account today. In this account, we meet a character named Bartimaeus who is blind but goes to Jesus with a deep longing to see. It is the one thing he wants more than anything else in the world. In the gospel, Jesus praises Bartimaeus's faith—Bartimaeus's capacity to lean into his longing with hope. And Jesus grants Bartimaeus's request.

At an initial glance, this might look like a story of physical healing, but throughout Christian history, the blindness and sight talked about in this story have been understood as a metaphor for something deeper. We get a clue into this deeper meaning from the name Bartimaeus. If you think about it, most of those whom Jesus heals don't have names, and Bartimaeus is a strange name. It is composed of the Hebrew word *bar*—which means "son of"—and the Greek name Timaeus. An unusual cross-cultural combination. Some scripture scholars suggest that when we hear the name, we are meant to remember another ancient character named Timaeus from the philosopher Plato's *Dialogues*. Timaeus is the character who tries to understand all that was known about the creation of the world and the elements that make up the universe. And, intriguingly, Timaeus is the character who describes sight as the beginning of knowledge.

The biblical Bartimaeus—son of Timaeus—turns to Jesus desiring physical sight, yes, but more than that, he represents the profound longing within each of us to know the world as it really is. He desires what we might call in the broader philosophical tradition "truth." And the point of this gospel passage is that, for the one who is willing to lean into that longing, for the one who doesn't back away from mystery but continues to live in hope, Jesus opens the door and makes understanding possible. Jesus can put you in contact with reality.

We live in a time that questions the value of truth, that questions the value of seeing things as they really are. We live in a time that wonders whether being accepted, comfortable, or entertained is really as much as one should hope for in life. A time that even goes so far to suggest that a virtual life—an imaginary life—would be a more desirable way of being in the world. That all of life could be constructed as a show. And there is pressure to remain silent and satisfied to live in such times. After all, there are coins coming into our cups each day, aren't there? As we are reminded on the news, the economy is generally good. It's not a bad life, is it?

But, knowing you, I suspect you'd tell me it's not enough. Deep down, there's a son of Timaeus in you and a son of Timaeus in me. There is someone who wants to try to understand the world and the elements that make up the universe. Cup of coins be damned. There is someone who wants to know what's real and to be in contact with what's real. And from way down inside, there is a voice that wells up in each of us gathered in this church tonight and cries out, "Jesus, son of David, have pity on me. I want to see! Do you hear me, Jesus? More than anything I want to see!"

If you have found that longing, that *deepest of human longings*, within you—take courage. Jesus has heard you. Indeed, he's calling for you. You, Bartimaeus, are the kind of person that he has come for. He can't promise you acceptance; he can't promise you comfort; he can't even promise you endless excitement. But *seeing*, well, *that* he can do. That longing twisted into your DNA has been placed there from the beginning of time for this moment in time, that it might bring you face to face with him. That longing is for the sake of your salvation. And you are now standing in the space where miracles can happen. Indeed, you should expect nothing less.

IF I MIGHT BE WRONG, THEN WHY BELIEVE ANYTHING?

We closed the last section by acknowledging that if truth is objective, by definition it means that we might be wrong about some things. Many contemporary hearers, preachers, and teachers alike find this realization haunting: "If there is always the chance that I might be wrong, then why bother to believe anything at all?"

All of us are occasional skeptics. We hear something and we think, "Huh, I'm not sure that's true." Doubt in itself is not a bad thing. We *should* ask hard questions of ourselves and others about why we believe the things we do. Pope Francis makes this very point: "We do not need to be afraid of questions and doubts because they are the beginning of a path of knowledge and going deeper; one who does not ask questions cannot progress either in knowledge or in faith."[4] Doubt becomes problematic, however, if it is not the beginning of a path but rather the end, a way of life in itself.

Skepticism as a way of life doesn't doubt that there *is* such a thing as reality, but it *so* emphasizes our potential to make mistakes about the nature of reality that it questions whether we can really know *anything*. Moreover, it suggests that if we can't know anything for certain, then the quest for truth is inherently misguided. It's not even worth it to try. In contrast to Bartimaeus, it lacks faith that sight is still possible. Truth stops being an objective: "I thought such and such was true, but then I found out this piece of information and everything got turned upside down. How do I know that I am not wrong again now? Who can I trust? I can't even trust myself. Why bother to keep thinking about this? I give up." Sometimes followed by "I'm outta here."

The problem with the skeptic's stance is that if one requires absolute certainty in order to believe anything, it becomes difficult to act. To use an example favored by the philosopher Ludwig

Wittgenstein, imagine if every morning you woke up and had to wonder, "Do I really have two hands or is that just a figment of my imagination?" We are able to move through our day only because there are some things we accept as certain.[5] If we were not able to have some basic trust in our ability to know reality, we wouldn't know when to plant crops; we wouldn't be able to travel by map; we wouldn't be able to cross the street. In short, we wouldn't be able to make the judgments needed to survive. Sure, there are times when we will make mistakes, times when the usual patterns of reality will throw us for a loop, but we can't allow that to deter us from still trying to understand.

In August 2017, I was one of those fortunate enough to be in the path of totality during the solar eclipse. It was amazing beyond anything I had expected. However, as soon as it was over, I found myself wondering, "What would this day have been like if I had not been led to expect anything out of the ordinary at all?" The last time a total eclipse had passed over my part of the country was 1442, fifty years before Columbus sailed the ocean blue. In a time before extensive travel and communication, the vast majority of people in the region probably had no idea such an event was imminent. One day they would have been out on the plains and suddenly the sun would have dimmed in the middle of the day. Bats, birds, crickets, and frogs would have launched into their nighttime routines. The stars would have appeared. A ring of fire would have burned in the darkened sky. And then three minutes later everything would have returned to normal. Is it any wonder so many ancient civilizations associated eclipses with outbreaks of sudden blindness? Given such an event, I, too, would have stared directly into the sun. And I would have continued staring at it for the remainder of the day—and weeks to follow—wondering, "Did I really just see that?"

Afterward, I imagine such an event would lead some to throw their hands in the air in despair: "We can't count on anything anymore! Who knows what will happen next?!" Most probably considered it a bizarre anomaly marking a divine omen or event but didn't allow it to change their understanding of how the world normally works. (We have countless eclipse myths from around the world testifying to this.) But we know that at least some sat with their experience—denying neither what they had seen that strange day nor how they knew the world to work—and held those two in tension with one another until they were able to figure out a mental picture of reality that was large enough for both. They waited in hope for clarity while living with the ambiguity.

A healthy response to skepticism favors that third response. Thomas Aquinas was very optimistic about the human ability to grasp reality. He emphasized that God has not created the world to play tricks on us. Rather, God *wants* the world to be known. And so God created human beings in such a way that we could genuinely encounter the world through our senses—sight, hearing, taste, smell, touch—and then, through the God-given gift of reason, gradually *make sense* out of those encounters. It doesn't mean that sometimes our senses won't deceive us.[6] And it doesn't mean that sometimes reality in its immensity won't toss us stuff that resembles nothing our senses have ever encountered before. When that happens, however, it isn't cause to throw up our hands in despair but rather to remain curious and open to learning.

The scriptures and saints of the liturgical calendar offer countless examples of persons who learned to live with ambiguity and maintain a sense of ongoing openness to truth even in the midst of breathtaking surprises and mystifying events. Abraham and Sarah only mark the beginning of a whole litany of holy men and women who could be lifted up in preaching and teaching as models of persons who had every reason to become skeptics but didn't. In the preaching that follows, I lift up Mary of Nazareth as one of these models, highlighting her capacity to take in confusing events and "ponder them in her heart."

Preaching Sample:
ON MARY'S HEART

FEAST OF THE IMMACULATE HEART OF MARY

SCRIPTURE TEXT: LUKE 2:41–51

Each year [Jesus'] parents went to Jerusalem for the feast of Passover, and when he was twelve years old, they went up according to festival custom. After they had completed its days, as they were returning, the boy Jesus remained behind in Jerusalem, but his parents did not know it. Thinking that he was in the caravan, they journeyed for a day and looked for him among their relatives and acquaintances, but not finding him, they returned to Jerusalem to look for him. After three days they found him in the temple, sitting in the midst of the teachers, listening to them and asking them questions, and all who heard him were astounded at his understanding and his answers. When his parents saw him, they were astonished, and his mother said to him, "Son, why have you done this to us? Your father and I have been look-ing for you with great anxiety." And he said to them, "Why were you looking for me? Did you not know that I must be in my Father's house?" But they did not understand what he said to them. He went down with them and came to Nazareth, and was obedient to them; and his mother kept all these things in her heart.

Today's gospel reading seems a bit of an anomaly, given that we are in the month of June. It is one that we usually associate with the Christmas season. But it is where it is because today in the Church we celebrate the Feast of the Immaculate Heart of Mary, and this passage illumines something of Mary's heart.

Devotion to the hearts of Jesus and Mary first became popular in France in the early 1600s in association with the French School of Spirituality and names such as St. John Eudes, St. Margaret Mary Alacoque, and St. Louis-Marie de Montfort. At a time following the Council of Trent, when the Church became tangled in heady doctrinal debates and repeatedly expressed itself in a series of anathemas, this spiritual movement highlighted anew the personal love that God has for each and every individual, and the intense affection and love each person is invited to share with God. In some way, we could say that the image of the Sacred Heart of Jesus intends to offer insight into the love of God for humans; and the image of the immaculate heart of Mary intends to offer insight into the way we as humans are to love God back.

Meeting Mary in the gospels—especially in the infancy narratives of Luke—there is much that we might be able to surmise about Mary's heart:

- It was an open heart—ready to do whatever God asked.
- It was a courageous heart—ready to leave the familiarity of Nazareth to traverse the mountains of Judea to visit her cousin Elizabeth.
- It was a joyful heart—where the words of scripture churned until they found voice in the exuberant song we call the Magnificat.
- It was a strong heart—surviving the terrors of giving birth in a barn far from home.

But there are only two times in the gospels where Mary's heart is explicitly mentioned—once after the visit of the shepherds, and once in the passage we read today when Jesus is found in the Temple at the age of twelve. In both of these cases, the phrase is similar: "Mary kept all these things, reflecting on them in her heart" (Lk 2:19); "[Mary] kept all these things in her heart" (Lk 2:51).

When scripture speaks directly of Mary's heart, it describes it as a discerning heart, a reflective heart. It is a heart that doesn't understand everything right away as it happens but rather needs time for things to make sense. It is a heart that doesn't jump, doesn't overreact, doesn't demand immediate explanation, but let's things be for a while. It is a heart that is comfortable with mystery. The immaculate heart of Mary is, at its core, a patient heart.

And ultimately, as St. John Eudes and his French sojourners would remind us, this is a clue as to what *our own hearts* should look like. That's tough. For in our lives, as in Mary's life, days are often filled with surprises. So much happens that doesn't feel as if it makes sense. Mary dealt with an unexpected pregnancy, uninvited guests, a lost teen. It could just as easily be an unanticipated diagnosis, a layoff we never saw coming, shocking news in the diocesan paper, an accusation made against someone we trusted. I often respond to the surprises of life with sharpness—a flare of anger with demand for immediate explanation. I can be up in the wee hours of the morning wrestling with scenarios in my mind until they yield some clarity and peace. It's hard to recognize God's presence in the tangled mysteries of life and then to just allow those things to remain mysteries for a while. To be okay with things not all being congruent and making sense all the time.

The German poet Rainer Maria Rilke perhaps summarized the invitation of the immaculate heart best when he wrote, "Be patient toward all that is unsolved in your heart and try to love the questions themselves. . . . Do not now seek the answers which cannot be given you because you would not be able to live them. And the point is, to

live everything. Live the questions now. Perhaps you will then gradually, without knowing it, live along some distant day into the answer."[7]

Pray this feast day that in imitation of Mary, my heart might grow
more patient with its unsolved questions. And I will pray for yours.

MAYBE YOU'RE RIGHT. MAYBE I'M RIGHT. WHO'S TO JUDGE?

Most of us are also occasional relativists. Someone begins to quib-
ble with us at a party about the validity of something we hold dear
and—not wanting to get into an argument—we end the conversation . . . "Well, everyone's entitled to their own opinion" or "It's
true for me." When pushed on the matter, most of us don't really
hold that truth is relative. We just want to get out of the conversation without causing a scene or hurting the relationship. It is not
the battle hill we want to die on.

Relativism, however, can and has become a way of life for
many. In contrast to skepticism, which holds that reality exists but
doubts we can grasp it in any meaningful way, relativism doubts
that there *is* any such thing as an all-encompassing reality. Reality,
like beauty, exists merely in the eye of the beholder. If in skepticism
nothing is true because we cannot be absolutely certain, in relativism
everything is true so long as someone believes it. There is no standard
by which we can judge among truth claims. All perspectives must
be equally accepted.

The seeds of relativism can be traced back to the Sophists of
ancient Greece, particularly to the philosopher Protagoras, who
opens his book on the topic of truth with the statement "Man is
the measure of all things," and later notes, "Things are for every
man what they seem to be." The illogic of Protagoras's position
was first pointed out by his contemporary, Plato, who noted that

if Protagoras's idea that all truth is relative *was itself relative*, then it is just one more opinion among many equally true opinions and nothing to give much credence. On the other hand, if Protagoras meant for his idea to be taken as true, then there must be at least *one* truth (Protagoras's idea) that wouldn't be relative. As summarized again by the philosopher Michael Lynch, "Suppose I . . . announce that there is no such thing as truth per se, there is only truth-for-me or truth-for-you. A fair question to ask would be whether the statement I just made is true or just true for me."[8]

Given the ease with which relativism as a logical stance can be defeated, we might assume that those who espouse relativism still today—2,500 years after Plato—either haven't thought it through or they have another significant unaddressed concern to which they want to draw attention. Many modern relativists would acknowledge their underlying concern is tied to the history of colonialism. For many centuries, European explorers, upon encountering another culture that perceived reality radically different than they did, used such differences to justify their domination—sometimes even the enslavement or annihilation—of that culture. Recognizing the degree of violence, death, and cultural decimation that have so often occurred when two cultures collide, many sincerely ask, "Who is to say that one worldview is better than another? That there is just one right way of looking at life? Who's to say that monogamy is superior to polygamy? Or that covering women from head to toe is better than going topless?" Persons asking these questions are not so much intending to adopt relativism as a philosophical stance but rather issuing a plea for greater tolerance of diversity.

From a Christian perspective, the concerns raised by the history of colonialism are significant. Christian churches—including the Catholic Church—played an undeniable role in that history. As relates to the question of relativism, however, it might help us to make a distinction between *tolerance for diversity of facts, tolerance for diversity of judgment,* and *tolerance for diversity of preference.*

I think most would agree that relativism *in relation to preference* is largely unproblematic. I hold that lime-flavored La Croix is better than lemon. My husband disagrees. I say, "You are entitled to your own opinion on this matter." We agree to disagree, and the world goes on with little consequence. As one of my mentors is apt to say, "A difference that doesn't make a difference isn't much of a difference."

The relativism that Plato and fellow philosophers were most concerned about was relativism *in relation to facts*. Either the earth revolves around the sun or it doesn't. Facts are not matters of opinion, and when we pretend that they are, it can have devastating consequences, as noted earlier.

The stickiest area is relativism *in relation to judgments*. We often agree on the facts but differ in our assessment of which facts are the most important ones to pay attention to, and what we should do in response to those facts.

On one hand, given the atrocities of history and the harm we have done to one another because of our differences, a more widespread "live and let live" approach makes a lot of sense. Yet if every culture's—and we could extend that to every *person's*—way of doing things is equally acceptable, and there is no way of judging among different practices, there is also no hope for changing the status quo—a status quo that may also be negatively impacting people's lives. Take, for example, the age-old practices of foot binding, genital mutilation, honor killings, or slavery. Simply saying that "there is no way to judge" cuts off tough conversations too early—conversations that, if we care about a more just world, we need to continue to have.[9] My suspicion is that most people who identify with contemporary relativism's underlying concerns (versus Protagoras's) would actually agree that we should not remain judgment-free on every issue. The most difficult conversations occur when those involved cannot agree whether something is a matter of fact or judgment, or whether something is a matter of moral judgment or mere preference. Because this is such a large topic, we'll spend more time looking at it in chapter 2, and we'll consider ways of preaching related to this topic at that point. (See especially the preaching sample titled "Renewing the Mind" on page 68.)

For now, let's acknowledge that Christianity places a high value in remaining in tough conversations rather than sidestepping them. While allowing lots of leeway for diversity of preference, the Catholic tradition worries a good deal about "differences that *do* make a difference"—in essence, judgments that have an impact on other people's well-being. It likewise rejects the notion that facts are inconsequential for human flourishing. When things that matter are at stake, a Catholic response to relativism insists that we avoid saying, "Whatever," and instead say, "Let's keep talking and not just let this go," remaining optimistic that such conversations won't remain forever stymied. We may yet arrive at new insights.

A word of caution: Given the heightened concern around relativism in the writings of recent popes, many of us have taken to using the word quite casually in reference to a wide variety of differences, not only in relation to facts but also in relation to issues of judgment and even preference. Relativism certainly is a serious problem if we want to live truth. The problem is that the term is employed so indiscriminately, and the dangers associated with it painted so broadly, that hearing the preacher cry "Relativism!" has become synonymous with the little boy crying "Wolf!" In many situations, the label "relativist" has come to serve as a convenient dismissal for any voice with whom the preacher disagrees while sparing the preacher the hard work of addressing genuine concerns related to structural injustices and those who have suffered from them.

Relativism is an academic term and, as noted in the introduction, academic language is to be avoided in preaching unless the goal of the preaching is specifically to introduce a new term. If your primary aim in a particular preaching *is* to familiarize your congregation specifically with the concept of relativism, then use the term, but define what it means while being careful not to dismiss legitimate justice concerns. It is all too easy when preaching about relativism to reinforce an us/them mentality.

WHY IS REASON SO IMPORTANT?

You may have already noticed that in response to both skepticism and relativism, the Catholic tradition offers similar advice: "Don't give up the quest for truth because you are doubtful or uncomfortable. Hang in the conversation. Remain in the search." In both situations, this advice is grounded in a conviction that humans are given a capacity—the gift of reason—that can help them make progress on even the toughest of puzzles.

Thomas Aquinas suggests that our human capacity to reason is one of the ways that we are in the image and likeness of God. God wants us to be able to know the world as it really exists, and reason enables us to do that. Reason is God's way of helping us arrive at "the deep-down truth of things."[10] Not necessarily our first impression of things. Not how we'd *like* things to be. But "the deep-down truth of things" as they really are. Reason is the ability to take what we learn from our encounter with the world and systematically link our different experiences so that our thoughts form a coherent whole, helping us to function in the world.

For Aquinas, science is reason at its best. He understands the term broadly: a science is any systematically organized body of knowledge on a particular aspect of reality.[11] The methods for arriving at that knowledge will vary according to the aspect of reality that we are trying to grasp. So, for example, a biologist will have a different approach for studying living creatures than will a physicist who studies properties of matter and energy than will a theologian who sets her sights on understanding better the mystery of God. Methods that work in the physical sciences (e.g., observation and experimentation) won't be able to glean information about metaphysical realities (e.g., God and angels). In the end, however, the different sciences have nothing to fear from one another. They are all ways of trying to understand the same one immense reality. So, even if for a time it looks as if what is being discovered by the various sciences is in contradiction (e.g., theology and evolutionary science in the time of Darwin), eventually all truth is one. And, indeed, it is our common longing for that deep-down truth of things that helps makes *us* one. Reason makes authentic conversation between people possible and meaningful, regardless of gender, culture, or economic diversity. Without being able to appeal to reason to help us bridge our differences, we often have little else to resort to other than violence.

Religious leaders are sometimes guilty of creating a false dichotomy between faith and reason: "Don't follow your head on this matter, listen to God speaking in your heart"; or "Don't pay attention to what the doctors say, just have faith!" Such statements assume that the God who created the human mind is not the same God who created the human heart, and that the God who set up the laws that govern the universe is a different God than the one we meet in prayer. Furthermore, many homilies ask congregations to believe incredulous things that, while part of the greater Catholic lore, are neither essential nor required tenets of the faith. For some congregants, hearing such stories presented as true feeds their spirit, but for others it is a distraction and makes it more difficult to believe what is core to the faith. As far back as the sixteenth century, the Fifth Lateran Council begged preachers to stop preaching on "imminent events, apocalyptic messages, preposterous stories, fabulous miracles, arcane trivia, heretical opinions, and downright nonsense."[12] Unfortunately the council's teaching bears repeating in the twenty-first century.

If we want contemporary hearers to live truth, we need to explicitly affirm that faith and reason ultimately live in harmony with one another. Not all scientists are friends of faith, but science itself is friend, not foe. In preaching, highlight the feasts of those who pursued holiness through dedication to science—be it biology, theology, psychology, or computer science. Encourage vocations to the sciences. Extol the study of science as a way to do truth in the world and as a path to finding God. Avoid categorizing scholars as "elites" disconnected from everyday folk. The following preaching is an attempt to honor the magi as precursors of modern scientists and highlights how their close observation of the natural world led them closer to God, not further away.

Preaching Sample:
OBSERVE THE STAR RISING

FEAST OF EPIPHANY

SCRIPTURE TEXT: MATTHEW 2:1–12

When Jesus was born in Bethlehem of Judea, in the days of King Herod, behold, magi from the east arrived in Jerusalem, saying, "Where is the newborn king of the Jews? We saw his star at its rising and have come to do him homage." When King Herod heard this, he was greatly troubled, and all Jerusalem with him. Assembling all the chief priests and the scribes of the people, he inquired of them where the Messiah was to be born. They said to him, "In Bethlehem of Judea, for thus it has been written through the prophet:

'And you, Bethlehem, land of Judah,
    are by no means least among the rulers of Judah;
since from you shall come a ruler,
    who is to shepherd my people Israel.'"

Then Herod called the magi secretly and ascertained from them the time of the star's appearance. He sent them to Bethlehem and said, "Go and search diligently for the child. When you have found him, bring me word, that I too may go and do him homage." After their audience with the king they set out. And behold, the star that they had seen at its rising preceded them, until it came and stopped over the place where the child was. They were overjoyed at seeing the star, and on entering the house they saw the child with Mary his mother. They prostrated themselves and did him homage. Then they opened their treasures and offered him gifts of gold, frankincense, and myrrh. And having been warned in a dream not to return to Herod, they departed for their country by another way.

All around the world today Christians celebrate what is popularly known as the Feast of the Three Kings. Of course, Matthew's gospel— the original source of the "three kings" story—never calls them kings, nor delineates their number as three. Matthew names them as "magi."

It's a term we don't hear much anymore, but at the time the gospels were written, *magi* was a word used in the wider Greco-Roman world to refer to the Zoroastrian priestly community in a part of the world we now know as Iran or Iraq. Their scholarship of the natural world, particularly the stars and planets, was so extensive that they were regarded across the Middle East as persons of extraordinary vision and special powers. Indeed, we can trace the roots of our word *magician* back to this community. But rather than think of them as sorcerers, it is probably more accurate to think of them as ancient astronomers—early scientists who dedicated their lives to watching the skies and were curious about what changes in the skies might mean for those of us who live on Earth. They were considered seers not because they had secret visions others did not have but because they paid such close attention to what is before all of our eyes yet so few of us take the time to observe.

The gospel account makes me wonder: How long and how closely must these particular magi have watched the skies in order to notice some sort of astronomical phenomenon that everyone else around them seems to have missed?[13] And how curious must they have been that they would travel somewhere in the vicinity of *a thousand miles* just to find out what that particular "rising star" meant? No cloudy crystal ball resting on a red velvet cushion for these guys. These magi had grit.

It's interesting that, according to Matthew's gospel, the magi's journey takes them first to Jerusalem. If they thought the rising of a new star indicated the birth of a new king, perhaps the palace in Jerusalem seemed the most likely place to find him. Everyone makes hypotheses based on previous experience, don't they? But it turns out that the palace was not to be their final destination. Their observations and their curiosity could take them so far, but what they still needed were the words of the prophets to point them in the right direction for the last leg of their journey. The magi rely both on science and scripture—working not in competition with each other but in harmony.

Equally interesting, however, is the role that Herod and his crew plays in this story. Theirs is a community that has the scriptures but seems to lack capacity for observation and curiosity. It is as if they have been gifted with the answer but have forgotten the question. So, while the magi depart from Jerusalem to "go and search diligently for the child," Herod himself remains seated on his red velvet cushion. The magi continue their thousand-mile trek, but Herod is not curious enough to join them for the final five miles from Jerusalem to Bethlehem to see for himself. "When you have found him, bring me word," he commands. Scripture, yes, he has that; but not one ounce the spirit of a scientist. Indeed, he sees their quest as dangerous. As threatening the status quo.

So often in our modern world, when I hear stories in the news, it seems as if scientific pursuit and religious faith are caricatured as opposing options and we are asked to ally with one or the other. Some say it's impossible nowadays to be a scientist who also is part of a faith community. Some say they've never met a religious person who remains curious and open to pursuing tough questions.

If you've ever had people say things like this to you, I hope today's gospel makes clear that you don't need to choose either science or faith. You don't have to pit astronomy and scripture against each other. As Catholics, we recognize that reason and faith complement each other. That close observation of the natural world coupled with rigorous curiosity is a path that we can trust will lead us closer to God, not further away. When we are fearful and afraid of upsetting the status quo, we will be tempted to perch on our own red velvet cushions and look at others who have traveled different paths with suspicion. But when we love and seek truth, wherever and however it is found, we find all paths merge, eventually leading to the same place.

The Gospel of Matthew is clear about who it would have us feasting with today, and it is not Herod, at home in his palace. It is the magi—those seekers from the East, who, upon having their curiosity struck by the rising of a new star, will not stop searching for its meaning, no matter how far they must travel. And pursuing truth wherever it leads, in whatever form it comes, they arrive at the place genuine seekers always inevitably seem to end up: face to face with God.

Are There Limits to Seeking Truth?

If the pursuit of truth is a sure path to God, it raises a question: Are there any limits to this quest? Is learning more *always* good? Is science ever a foe? Here we'd have to acknowledge that in all of the Christian life we have to guard against the extremes.

It is interesting to note that curiosity is not traditionally listed as a Christian virtue. Indeed, Augustine of Hippo and Thomas Aquinas name *curiositas* as a vice. Augustine described it as "concupiscence of the eyes,"[14] and Aquinas saw it as an offense against temperance.[15] But the *curiositas* about which they were concerned is something quite different than the curiosity generally associated with the sciences. Augustine was referring to a curiosity that drew his attention to lurid theater and public scandals. Aquinas was warning against knowledge sought merely for the sake of puffing oneself up to look good or pursued at the cost of more profitable activities. (Although Facebook and Twitter did not exist in his day, these are the types of curiosities that he seems to have had in mind.) Contrast this with the wonder of the magi whose curiosity was motivated by a desire to understand creation better.

But even with regard to pursuit of the sciences, we need to acknowledge limits. Perhaps the greatest story of caution can be found in the earliest chapters of Genesis, where God tells the first humans that they are "free to eat from any of the trees in the garden except the tree of knowledge of good and evil" (Gn 2:16–17). It seems like such an odd prohibition. Why wouldn't God want people to have knowledge of what is good and what is evil? It might help if we were to consider the original Hebrew meaning of this text. "Good and evil" is a common Hebrew figure of speech, similar to "heaven and earth," in which two opposites are juxtaposed in order to try to convey "and everything in between." So, in this situation, the storyteller is trying to say "knowledge of *everything*." Furthermore, in Hebrew, "knowledge" is often a euphemism for intimate or sexual knowledge.[16] From a Jewish perspective, this text is often interpreted as God setting sexual experience off limits for the new human beings if they want to be immortal (i.e., eat from the "tree of life").

One way of pondering this passage is to consider that God's limitation may not have necessarily been intended for all time but that—fresh from the clay of the earth—humans simply weren't ready for all knowledge yet. While in artwork we often conceive of Adam and Eve as full-grown adults, their portrayal in Judaism and early Christianity often paints them as children. There is knowledge out there that they are not prepared to handle.

Once, when studying this passage with a group of preteens, I asked if there were things that they had seen that they wished they had not yet seen, and almost all answered in the affirmative. They had glimpsed scenes of sex, violence, terror—good and evil and everything in between—that they didn't have the internal capacity to make sense of at this stage in their development. Eventually it would be good and important to know the truth about these things, but not yet. We need to balance our external search for the truth of the world with a concurrent internal maturation process that will enable us to wisely handle what we discover about reality. One of the great challenges we face is discerning how to assist in this maturation process in the young people to whom we speak on behalf of the Church. What is the right age at which to begin to talk about the beauty of sex, for example? How about the reality of sexual abuse?

Many of us would acknowledge that even as adults, there is information becoming available to us that we as a species are not yet mature enough to handle with appropriate care. Many ethicists would include here things such as how to split an atom, CRISPR technologies, and embryonic stem cell research. Should we continue to pursue technical knowledge that has the potential to do irreparable harm to us as a species?

Finally, it needs to be said that there may be some knowledge we are never meant to have, no matter how old or ethically mature we grow, because the only way that we would be able to come by such knowledge is by evil means. Consider the medical experiments conducted in Nazi concentration camps by physicians such as Josef Mengele in which Jewish and Roma prisoners were intentionally subjected to horrible diseases and extreme conditions in order to study systematically the limits of human endurance.[17] Or consider the Tuskegee experiment conducted between 1932 and 1972 during which 399 African American men were withheld treatment for syphilis to see what the effects of the disease on the body would be if left untreated.[18] As people charged with advocating the seeking of truth, we want to acknowledge also that there are some things we as humans are simply not meant to know because in order to find them out, we would have to engage in sin.

A SUMMARY OF CHAPTER 1

Living in a post-truth society raises urgent questions for contemporary Christians: What is truth? Why should I care? How can I know? What can I do if someone else's truth is different from my own? Isn't that just something we have to live with? Is there any way for us to break through our differences? While previous generations certainly asked these questions as well, they have become a source of discouragement, even despair, for many in the present context. Part of announcing the Good News in this particular time involves proclaiming a word of hope regarding these fundamental questions related to truth, reminding hearers that the Catholic tradition:

- affirms that there is such a thing as reality and that, while it is immense and beyond anything we could grasp in its totality,

God has created the universe with the intention that it be known by us;

- names truth (having a mind aligned with reality) as essential for our survival and thriving, and ultimately for enjoying God;
- expresses concern with the skeptic's claim that just because we can't know everything, we can't know anything;
- expresses concern with the relativist's claim that just because someone believes something, it must be somehow true;
- proposes reason as a gift from God that we are meant continually to develop in order to break through situations of impasse and come to greater truth; and
- honors systematic study (the sciences) as a noble pursuit through which humans exercise their God-given call to grow in truth.

While these points seem very basic, they are the foundational building blocks for reconstructing a holistic sensibility around truth in our present context. If our communities are going to be able to live truth in any of the other realms that we will discuss in the chapters to follow, it is helpful if these concepts are already in place. Fortunately the liturgical year, with its many feasts and memorials, offers abundant opportunity to explore these foundational points and models of life that embody them. Our challenge is to explore these tenets in such a way that it attracts hearers rather than makes them feel ignorant for questioning them in the first place. We want to do all we can to make truth a desirable and viable lifestyle—something we want for ourselves and something we believe possible.

For Reflection and Dialogue

- What is your relationship to truth in your personal life? How have you defined it up to this point? Do you love truth above all else and see the pursuit of truth as an essential part of your spiritual journey? How do you see *yourself* falling prey to paradigms of skepticism, relativism, or dichotomizing faith and reason?

- What do you sense to be some of the biggest quandaries around truth in your particular congregation? How have people in your community struggled—explicitly or implicitly—with the questions addressed in this chapter? How do they express the struggle? Around what kinds of issues have these questions surfaced?

- How would you assess the effectiveness of the preaching samples in this chapter in terms of the five markers of effectiveness named in this book's introduction: having a single message; using a conversational tone; specificity in language; valuing autonomy; and anticipating diversity of perspectives? What do you think would heighten the samples' effectiveness?

- As a church leader, when is the last time that you tried to address a question related to truth? How did it go? What might you try differently the next time around?

- What makes you most nervous about trying to address some of these questions in the current climate? What kind of resistance do you experience, if any, around drawing attention to these topics in preaching, teaching, and leading? Is there anything that would persuade you to give it a try? If so, where might you start?

2.

Truth

AS A WAY OF FORMING GOOD JUDGMENTS

In the first chapter I introduced living truth in relation to the classical definition of the term: always striving to have one's mind be in alignment with reality. When we talk about truth in this way, we are asking questions related to the existence and nature of things. We are trying to find out what is and what is not. Nothing in the universe half exists. Either you were born in the state of Indiana or you were not. Either Earth is 4.6 billion years old or it is not. In common parlance, there is no way to be "a little bit pregnant." Additional information might change our understanding of *how* something is true. For instance, Aristotle, Isaac Newton, and Albert Einstein each hypothesized how gravity works differently, but none of them doubted that gravity *is*. Doing truth, at this most foundational level, is about making sure that we have the best grasp possible of what would widely be referred to as "the facts."

The human mind, however, does more than simply collect facts, which often can be verified, rejected, or refined based on observation and logic. The mind also collates facts, organizing them in such a way that they make sense to us as a whole. The mind uses what it has gleaned from the world to arrive at statements such as:

- It's true that gambling is wrong.
- The fact of the matter is no one should drive drunk.
- That judge is racist—you can't deny it.
- As a matter of fact, we had plenty of kids to merit keeping the parish school open.

Even though these are also truth claims, these beliefs are of a different nature than belief in gravity or quarks. It is hard to tell the difference in the midst of a conversation, because the language is so similar. But these statements are not so much about whether or how something exists but whether something is good or bad. They are about whether someone should or shouldn't. Whether this is better than that. Even when we label them as facts, these are not facts; they are judgments—or we might also say opinions, conclusions, or convictions—that people hold as true.

To say that something is an opinion is not to say that it's not true but rather that it's true (or not) in a different way. May I suggest that you read that last sentence twice? It's an important one and not easy to grasp. We are now talking about truth as it pertains to meaning making and decision-making, and we don't want to mix apples and oranges. We often do, including in the acts of preaching and teaching. The conflation of fact and judgment is a good part of what makes talking about truth in a post-truth society feel so hopeless and stuck. But we take a step in a helpful direction when we make a critical distinction: While reality itself is objective, the person who tries to make sense of it and to figure out what to do in the middle of it is always a subject, a unique individual who is shaped by the particularities of life and circumstance, including personal experiences, family of origin, geography of home, culture with its native tongue, specific desires and feelings, differing degrees of formal education, and the like. And each of the above factors into the way that a person makes meaning of and judges the world, making truth claims of this nature often more difficult to adjudicate than truth claims related to facts. (And Galileo thought *he* had it tough!)

WHAT ALL GOES INTO THE MAKING OF AN OPINION?

I acknowledge up front that this is *not* a question currently being asked by most congregations, but we as Church leaders want to explore it anyway, because without considering how opinions are formed, the other questions related to judgment will prove quite challenging to address. Indeed, if we could stir an interest in this question among hearers, I suspect half of the conversations they currently find so frustrating could easily be resolved. A most helpful framework for beginning to explore the question is the work of the late Harvard Business School professor Chris Argyris, who in the 1970s constructed a model called the "ladder of inference" to describe the process that the human mind goes through in order to arrive at the opinions it holds about the world.[1]

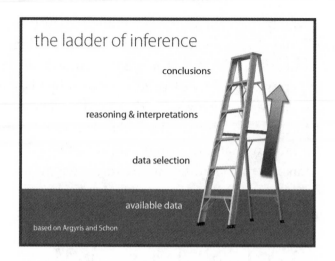

At the base of Argyris's model exists all of the data—or facts—that are available to me. This lowest level of the model parallels what we described in chapter 1 as objective reality. Recall that what is available to me is not the totality of all the data that exists on this matter. Others may have access to data that I do not, and all of us together will likely still not know all that could be known on any matter.

But even of the data that is available to me, Argyris's model points out that my mind only pays attention to some of it. Why? Because the data I could be paying attention to is immense and overwhelming! Moreover, life has taught me that only some of it is necessary to pay attention to. How did I learn that lesson? Life experiences, especially while growing up.

Early on, for instance, I learned it was more important to listen to the voice of the teacher in the front of the room than to count the number of tiles on the classroom floor, watch the fly buzzing around in the air, or spy Amy and Melissa passing notes behind me. Paying attention to one set of data points earned me an A in class. Paying attention to another set of data points could land me in the principal's office. So, over the course of a lifetime, I was repeatedly socialized by family, friends, educational systems, work cultures, religious communities, and more to unconsciously privilege the voice of authority in the front of the room more than the other things going on within the same space. Most of the time I am unaware that I am doing so. In my own mind, I am just paying attention to the facts that matter. I am simply noticing what is important.

Once my brain has selected data to pay attention to, it begins to assign meaning and interpretation to the data, again based on what the particularities of my own life experience and cultural context have previously taught me. For example, if I go outside to the church parking lot after a spring rainstorm, I could pay attention to the puddles on the ground or I could pay attention to the sky. In essence, experience may have taught me to privilege looking in one direction over the other, especially if I've soaked my feet previously in surprise puddles. But let's say that my eyes are on the sky, and I see a rainbow. Based again on my own background, I might think to myself, "What an amazing meteorological phenomenon caused by the refraction of light on water droplets!" Or I might think to myself, "Genesis. God set his bow in the sky." Because I've been coloring pictures of Noah and the ark since I was four, and I did just come from church after all, let's say the rainbow reminds me of the biblical account.

When I step in my front door, I share my conclusion with my brother: "You know what? Everything is going to be okay in the world. We should have hope." And he, sodden and wet, having spotted only a hint of rainbow before a nearby car drove through a puddle the size of Lake Michigan, is utterly puzzled from whence this grand proclamation suddenly emerged.

The ladder of inference helps to explain not only how the mind arrives at conclusions but also why different minds arrive at different conclusions. It helps to explain why a group of people—all sincerely open to reality and endowed with the gift of reason—could still end up holding very different truths. In many disagreements, it turns out that we *do* agree on the facts. What we disagree about is which facts matter, which facts we should pay attention to and which ones are less relevant, what the facts mean, and how they should be interpreted.

Although Argyris's model was not designed to capture Catholic intuitions about how the brain arrives at judgments, it aligns nicely. Thomas Aquinas similarly observed, "Even though the sense always apprehends a thing as it is unless there is an impediment in the organ or in the medium, the imagination usually apprehends a thing as it is not."[2] Aquinas affirms that, unless we have some sort of physical or mental deficiency, it is not our ability to grasp the world through our senses that is the source of our differences of perception. The challenge lies at the level of our imagination—the way that we form the facts into pictures in our minds.

Even though each of us has an abundance of experience, history, culture, family story, and more shaping our imagination, the lower rungs of our ladders often go unexplored in our personal reflection, our conversations with one another, and our preaching and teaching. In a fast-paced world where we are under pressure to make choices quickly, we tend to exchange words with each other only from the top rungs of our respective ladders: "Let me tell you what's true." This results in a frustrating back-and-forth argument, as you try to persuade me to share your conclusion and I try to persuade you to share mine. It is as if we each want others to make a leap ten feet above the ground from the top of their ladder to the top of ours, when experience suggests that the only way a wise person would shift from the top of one ladder to another would be by descending the rungs of their own ladder one by one and then ascending the rungs of the other one by one.[3]

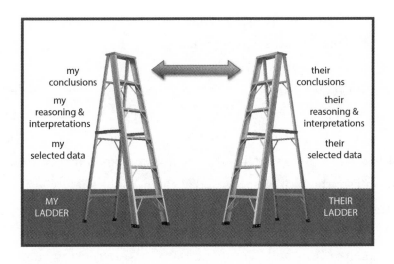

In the retreat preaching that follows, I share an example from my own life that uses (implicitly) the ladder of inference as a tool for breaking open a hasty conversation with my husband from which I had much to learn. I do so with the goal of inviting hearers to consider their own opinions and to illustrate how asking different questions can lead us to a deeper exploration of what each of us holds as true—a theme picked up again later in this chapter.

Preaching Sample:
THE EAR OF THE WISE
SCRIPTURE TEXT:
PROVERBS 18:1–2, 6, 13, 15

One who is alienated seeks a pretext, with all persistence picks a quarrel. Fools take no delight in understanding but only in displaying what they think. . . . The lips of fools walk into a fight, and their mouths are asking for a beating. . . . Whoever answers before listening, theirs is folly and

shame. . . . The heart of the intelligent acquires knowledge,
and the ear of the wise seeks knowledge.

Recently after watching a feature story in the news on the challenges of interracial dialogue, a memory resurfaced in my mind. It involved an incident that I'd not thought about for over twenty years—an incident that had taken place shortly after my husband and I moved from the beautiful southern tip of the island of Guam to the slightly less exotic southern tip of the city of St. Louis, Missouri.

We had awoken this particular morning to find a fresh layer of snow blanketing the lawn of the flat we were renting, and I was thrilled. As we looked out from our second-story window, I could see that someone—probably a neighborhood kid—had already been traipsing about on the lawn. I went to bundle up our toddler so that he could join in the fun. My husband turned to me and said, "What are you doing? You can't take him out there. It's dangerous."

"It's dangerous to play in snow?" I asked, befuddled. Granted, he grew up in Guam, but surely he knew that people played in snow.

"Someone has carved KKK into our lawn!" he exclaimed.

I was even more befuddled. Admittedly there were lines like chicken scratch in the snow. Maybe they looked like a *K*. Maybe two *K*'s. Or maybe they looked like the traces of a neighborhood child dragging a stick.

Sometimes I can't help myself. *The lips of fools walk into a fight.*

"You think that someone from a hate group came and carved two-thirds of their name into our front lawn?" I asked.

"They were clearly in the middle of doing so when probably someone spotted them and they ran away," he replied.

"That's ridiculous," I told him. *Whoever answers before listening, theirs is folly and shame.* He walked away.

Which of us was right? There really was no way of telling. The only person who would know is the person who made the marks in the snow (assuming they were of a sentient age), and that person was nowhere to be found. So, twenty years ago, the conversation ended there.

Neither of us spoke of the incident again, and I'd long assumed that my husband had forgotten about it after realizing how preposterous his idea was. But a few weeks ago, after watching the news feature, I asked him, "Do you remember that time when we had just moved to St. Louis and it snowed?" He replied, "You mean that time when someone wrote 'KKK' on our lawn?" He had not forgotten. Wow.

And so twenty years later, we talked. The good news is that an additional twenty years of marriage has taught us a few things. It's brought us to the point where the book of Proverbs no longer feels like the unwanted advice of our parents and instead feels more like common sense.

In twenty years we've come to discover that "Who is right?" may be an interesting conversation to have . . . for about, oh, say, five minutes. But that even when we disagree about the answer to that question—which for both of us remains, "Me!"—there are other questions worth asking, other conversations to be had. As Proverbs says, "The ear of the wise seeks knowledge."

And so tonight I want to name three ways we can practice wisdom with our ears. I'm sure you know these already, for surely you have been around the block a few times in your own relationships as well. But sometimes it can be helpful to organize what we've learned in easy-to-remember ways, which is what the book of Proverbs really is all about, isn't it? So, here we go:

One: We practice wisdom with our ears when we listen for another's logic.
That sounds a little lofty, so let me give an example of what I mean. In my version of the story, I think my husband is off his rocker. But in his version of the story, my husband would never say, "You know why I believe what I do? It's because I'm off my rocker." In his head, he holds what he believes to be a reasonable conclusion that makes sense. If he didn't believe it made sense, he wouldn't believe it. So, the more important question isn't "Who's right?" but "Why do we each see this so differently?"[4] Is it because we each have access to some information that the other doesn't have? Is it a question of us choosing different information as the information worth paying attention to? Does the difference lie in how we are interpreting the information? Any of these is a possibility.

I grew up in south St. Louis. I wanted to move back there because I remember my neighborhood as a friendly and safe place to raise a kid—the kind of place where children can still run freely up and down the block and drag sticks in the snow. I'd read about the KKK in history books, but I never thought of it in the present tense. My husband grew up in Guam. He was one of the only persons of color for blocks around. He had not found St. Louis to be warm and welcoming but suspicious and hesitant. He enjoyed watching the History Channel and thought of the KKK as something very much in the present tense. Practicing wisdom with our ears means trying to figure out why the story the other is telling makes sense to the other person based on their knowledge and experience.

Two: We practice wisdom with our ears when we listen for feelings.
Whether we agree with another's conclusions or not, we can listen to the feelings that lie underneath the story for this person. Seeing the marks in the snow was alarming for my husband. If I was in his shoes

and thought that someone was intentionally marking KKK into the lawn, I'd be frightened. I'd feel unwanted and outcast. I'd feel angry. I'd feel disgusted. I'd wonder why I had moved halfway around the world to live in a place that did these sorts of things. I'd want to go home.

One of the most helpful ways we can listen to another person is to name the feelings that undergird what they are saying. We want to do this gently. We never know exactly how another feels. The best we can say is, "It sounds as though you are feeling . . ." or "If it were me, I'd be feeling . . ." We want to be particularly careful not to tell someone how to feel. (In the history of time, "Calm down now" has never actually made someone feel calm.) But we can bring the conversation to a new level by affirming the feelings that people already have. A wise ear is not afraid of feelings but moves with courage into the realm of listening for another's emotions.

Three: We practice wisdom with our ears when we listen for meaning and importance.
The stories we tell, especially those that remain in our memory over a long period of time, are part of our life story. They often symbolize larger intangible themes in our lives. They represent something bigger to us. In the case of my husband, the marks in the snow were a sign of the repeated experiences he'd had since arriving in St. Louis six months earlier. They were something concrete he could point to representing the myriad times when he'd been made to feel unwelcome in the neighborhood: when people had crossed to the other side of the street with their dogs rather than walk past him; when cashiers eyed him with suspicion; when persons stopped him in the grocery aisle assuming he was a stocker rather than a shopper. It was important for him to tell me that there were aspects of his experience that I was not

privy to and he needed me to take those seriously rather than brush them aside by labeling them "ridiculous."

I wish that my ears had been wiser twenty years ago. Since that time, much more has been peeled back revealing racial tensions in the St. Louis area that I was blind to as a young adult. While I still doubt the intentionality of the marks in the snow, I don't know for certain that they were not intentional, and my husband's conclusion makes more sense to me now than it did then. Even though we will never know the origin of the marks, we have a different set of questions to ask each other now that has led to a more satisfying and meaningful conversation. I can acknowledge that, whether I like it or not, he's onto something regarding my beloved neighborhood. And he knows that, even though I'm not sure I agree, I've heard at a deeper level what he has to say.

So, here's a proverb to hang on to. It's not in the Bible, but I think it should be, for it is born of great wisdom and rings very true. I wish it was my wisdom. It's not. It is the wisdom of the Mennonite writer David Augsburger. Here it is: "Being listened to is so close to being loved that for the average person they are almost indistinguishable."[5]

It is worth saying once more: "Being listened to is so close to being loved that for the average person they are almost indistinguishable."

You'd agree, wouldn't you? If the sole aim of conversation is to figure out who's right, we end up having frustrating, truncated conversations. But if we listen as a way of trying to express love for another, we can discover marvelous new things about one another. Listen and love with your wise ears today.

Aren't We Entitled to Our Own Opinions?

Our lives as preachers, teachers, and leaders would be a lot easier if everyone in our congregations, classrooms, and boardrooms began to explore the question of truth in judgments from a reflective stance: "Why do I hold the opinions I hold? How did I form my judgments?" I suspect most instead approach from a confrontational stance: "Aren't I entitled to hold my own opinion?" It's a question that comes with a lot of embedded assumptions we'll need to handle with great care whenever we speak.

The ladder of inference helps explain why, even though we all live on the same planet, we still arrive at such different notions regarding how to live on it. What the ladder of inference doesn't help explain is what to *do* about the fact that we hold such different truths or beliefs. Some might say there is nothing that needs to be done about it. Each person is free to stand upon his or her own ladder. Each person is free to hold and act upon his or her own beliefs. Ultimately the Christian tradition affirms that statement (as we will discuss momentarily when we get to conscience) but not before adding a whole lot of nuance into the mix. Christianity also reminds us that as human beings, whether we want to be or not, we are part of a wider community. The tradition sees this as a good thing: God made us to be in relationship with God and others. It is only by living in community that we learn and grow and become who God dreams us to be. Yet it also means that our beliefs—and the actions that result from those beliefs—are going to impact God and others, whether we mean them to or not. As the seventeenth-century English poet John Donne wrote, "No man is an island."

Sometimes our differences in judgment don't matter much. I hold that my college alma mater is the best place ever. My son picked another university. My brother wanted their baby's room to be orange; my sister-in-law, green. Some differences in judgment are so minor that we might even label them (as we did in chapter 1) differences in preference. Negotiating such differences often involves compromising, flipping a coin, splitting the difference, or agreeing to do our own thing. The world is no worse for the wear. We might say that these judgments are of an amoral nature. They are not immoral. Rather, they are differences that don't make much of a difference in our ability to be in relationship.

In many cases, however, our differences in judgment *do* matter and each person doing their own thing is not inconsequential. Given how intertwined we are, even choices that seem highly personal—how I vote, how I drive, how much I drink—have implications for others' lives. I may not believe in immunizing my child and claim a right to make that choice for my family, but my child will cross paths in the world with your child while in school and on the playground. If your child is immune-compromised, my beliefs and the choices I make based upon those beliefs could endanger the life of your child. I may not believe humans contribute to climate change, but you and I both breathe the same air and depend upon the same water supply. Your health is also at stake.

When our truths have consequences for relationships, they become moral in nature. And so, even though it is very difficult to assess the truth of a judgment, we need some way of being able to do so in order to live on this planet with one another without erupting into violence—our age-old means of "resolving" consequential differences for which the world *is* worse for the wear. While everyone has opinions, some opinions are truer—or more *worthy*—than others.

Note the shift in our working definition of truth here. We are now striving for something different than we were in chapter 1. Previously our objective was to know reality. Practicing truth meant having a mind aligned with reality. In this chapter, our objective is to figure out what would be *best*. Practicing truth in this sense means *having a mind aligned with the greatest good*. And the quest for the good—like the quest for reality—comes with a well-worn map but still no step-by-step, foolproof guide.

The Catholic tradition has multiple ways of naming the greatest good that we are aiming for. Jesus called it "the kingdom of God." Ultimately we might simply name it "God." As we speak to congregations and classes who may be unfamiliar with the rich theological nuances behind each of those terms, perhaps the easiest door through which to enter a conversation about the Christian notion of "the good" is John 10:10, in which Jesus says, "I came so that they might have life and have it more abundantly." The greatest good is a flourishing of life. And so, when assessing the truth of moral belief, what we are in the broadest sense asking is, "Does holding this belief lead toward a greater flourishing of life or not?"

That's tricky, isn't it? Thomas Aquinas himself admitted as much. Aquinas noted that there were certain principles that all people of goodwill around the earth were inclined toward naturally as leading toward greater life, but he acknowledged that persons of goodwill might still come to different conclusions in concrete situations that involved the application of those principles—an exercise he referred to as "practical reason."[6]

It turns out that the worthiness of an opinion can't be measured with a ruler or verified by observations through a telescope. We will need to lift up a different set of commitments to help live truth with regard to the formation of judgments that impact others. There are three concepts from the tradition that I suggest we regularly integrate into our preaching and teaching in order to help our communities assess and strengthen their own processes of working up the ladder of inference to arrive at true conclusions.

Remain Grounded in Reality

As described in chapter 1, the Catholic tradition holds that there is such a thing as reality. Any judgment that we arrive at that doesn't have its footing in reality is bound to be a faulty judgment. If we do our diocesan planning based on recent census demographical information, and the census data is inaccurate, it doesn't matter how careful our interpretation of the data is; the opinion we arrive at will be less true than it could be. If we are trying to decide which particular cancer treatment to pursue, but our doctor has accessed erroneous research data, it doesn't matter which part of that data our doctor bases a recommendation on; the recommendation is less true than we want it to be. When working up the ladder of inference, before selecting the data we think worth paying attention to and trying to make sense of that data, we need to make sure we are working with real data. This is what makes "fake news" so dangerous in our time. We are forming judgments grounded in erroneous or absent data. Because reality is immense, it is always possible to learn additional facts, but by definition it is not possible to have "alternative facts."

Inform Your Conscience

In place of the American maxim "Everyone is entitled to their own opinion," the Catholic tradition upholds "Everyone must follow their own conscience." At first these two statements sound similar, but a closer look reveals them to be quite different.

Conscience, like reason, is a gift from God, a unique human capacity. While reason helps us align our mind with reality, conscience helps us align our mind with the good. It helps us distinguish in the core of our being between right and wrong. It helps us figure out what would be the greatest good in a particular situation and how to act on that good. *The Pastoral Constitution on the Church in the Modern World*—one of the most significant documents of the Second Vatican Council—says of conscience, "Its voice, ever calling them to love and to do what is good and to avoid evil, tells them inwardly at the right moment: do this, shun that" (*Gaudium et Spes* 16).

In Catholicism, conscience—similar to the American concept of opinion—is sacrosanct. It is to be respected, and no one
should be asked to violate their conscience. In that sense, we're
each "entitled" to act on our own conscience. But unlike the common notion of opinion, conscience is understood to be fallible.
The same document acknowledges that "conscience goes astray
through ignorance which it is unable to avoid," but also for "the
person who takes little trouble to find out what is true and good,
or when conscience is gradually almost blinded through the habit
of committing sin" (*Gaudium et Spes* 16). Hence, we are obligated
to make certain that our conscience is well formed. In addition to
listening to our own deep intuitions around what is right and good
in any situation, we must educate ourselves regarding the facts,
and we must be open to the wisdom of family, friends, colleagues,
and experts in the field. If Christian, we must consult scripture
and Church teaching. The individual freedom each of us has to
arrive at a belief and act upon it comes with the responsibility of
due diligence.

One of the things the ladder of inference makes clear is how
much our individual processes of arriving at judgments are influenced by factors of which we are barely aware in the moment—
our families of origin, our culture, our personality traits, and the
like. The Church's teaching about conscience asks us to wake up
to what is in the lower rungs of our ladder and become more
intentional about what filters we want data from the outside world
to pass through as our judgments are formed. As human beings
we are influenced and shaped by these environments. But we also
possess a capacity that no other creature seems to possess: the
ability to influence and shape our environments. We are both the
products of our cultures and the creators of our cultures.[7] We
can work to become increasingly aware of what lies in the middle
rungs of our ladder. We can ask if those influences are the ones
that we *want* to be shaping our data selection and interpretation.
By what we read, what news stations we watch, who we choose to

befriend, and how we decide to spend our time, we can change the way our mind filters and makes sense of information.

The Church's conviction is that intentionally forming our conscience, like intentionally developing our gift of reason, will lead us to greater unity with one another while still honoring our individuality. *The Pastoral Constitution* asserts, "Through loyalty to conscience, Christians are joined to others in the search for truth and for the right solution to so many moral problems which arise both in the life of individuals and from social relationships" (*Gaudium et Spes* 16).

Consider the Voice of Those Impacted

Subsidiarity may seem like an odd concept to be introducing in a chapter on pursuing truth in our judgments. As a principle in Catholic social teaching, it was given voice in the 1931 encyclical *Quadragesimo Anno* to encourage governments to give as much authority as possible to local communities, never taking on functions at the national level that could be handled just as well, or even better, at the local level.[8] The interest behind this principle, however, is that those who are most impacted by a decision should be the ones who have the most say in how it is made.

We see this interest at the very center of Jesus' ministry. Over and over again Jesus showed his concern for those negatively impacted by the way his own society was structured—widows, children, lepers. He spent a great deal of time talking with these people and making sure their concerns were heard and addressed. In his preaching he encouraged the Pharisees to become aware of the way that their rigid proclamations and judgments were impacting others, repeatedly asking them to take on a new perspective in the way they were reading situations. In the end of time, Jesus taught, we all will be judged by whether or not we attended to the cries of "the least" in our own choices.

The two preaching samples that follow highlight the second and third points raised in this section. Without ever using the term, "Renewing the Mind" invites reflection on what is often referred to as *moral relativism*—or relativism with regard to judgments. In contrast to the factual relativism we talked about in chapter 1—which questions whether we can name something as real or not—moral relativism questions whether we can name something as good or bad, right or wrong. Because judgment is so highly influenced by culture and personal experience, many preachers and other Church leaders acknowledge that moral relativism is a more difficult topic to address in a congregation. Those who think "You just have to tell people what is right and what is wrong" have not fully reckoned with the root causes of moral relativism, and as such, each time they "just tell people," they both ignore the congregation's need for appreciation and autonomy and create an us/them mentality (two of the marks of ineffective preaching identified in the introduction). Without meaning to, they unwittingly contribute to the mass exodus we have seen from our pews rather than helping to correct the problem. In order to get to the root of moral relativism, we need to address specifically and sensitively the underlying assumptions that open-mindedness is an end in itself and judgments—our own or those of others—shouldn't be challenged.

"Whose Voice Am I Missing?" invites hearers to reflect on whether their judgments take sufficient account of the impact their judgments have on others, especially those who are poor or marginalized. The passage of the Syrophoenician woman has similarities to the passage we considered in chapter 1 concerning Bartimaeus. In both cases, Jesus says that it is the person's faith that has made healing possible. In the earlier passage, Jesus seems to be referring to Bartimaeus's faith that, with Jesus, sight is still possible. In this passage, Jesus seems to be referring to the woman's faith that Jesus could and would change his mind.

===

Preaching Sample:
RENEWING THE MIND
TWENTY-SECOND SUNDAY IN ORDINARY TIME YEAR A

SCRIPTURE TEXT: ROMANS 12:1–2

I urge you therefore, brothers, by the mercies of God, to offer your bodies as a living sacrifice, holy and pleasing to God, your spiritual worship. Do not conform yourselves to this age but be transformed by the renewal of your mind, that you may discern what is the will of God, what is good and pleasing and perfect.

A renewal of the mind. That is what an engineer named Max was after when he left his job at Google a few years back.

I learned about Max from a podcast.[9] Apparently Max loved his job. Loved life in San Francisco. Loved the people he worked with. But as the months passed, Max began to realize that he was living in a "bubble." He was only meeting others who shared his experiences and reinforced his views. He decided that in order to broaden his perspective, he would design an app that would send him to random public events posted on Facebook, allowing him to meet and talk with people he would never otherwise encounter. The app took him to a gathering of young Russian professionals, a pancake breakfast, a salsa-dancing event, and even Christmas dinner at a stranger's home. Max admitted it could be incredibly awkward to go where the app sent him. After all, he didn't know anyone there. Sometimes it took him places where he didn't exactly feel safe, such as a biker bar on the side of a rural highway. But he would go in open-minded—not there to judge, just to meet people wherever they were at. It turned out that the experience was so enriching, he eventually quit his job to devote two years of his life to following where the app might take him across the country. He also began to share the app with others so that they could join in the experiment. Max and his colleagues continued to have amazing conversations that opened their eyes to the experiences of others and introduced them to very different activities than they would have otherwise enjoyed. Turns out bocce ball is super fun.

Bubbles were bursting all over the place. And as I was listening to the podcast, I found myself really admiring Max. One of the things the 2016 election illumined for so many of us was how small our bubbles are—how we only talk to people who are like us. We have few inter-racial friendships, few interreligious friendships. We know so little about other parts of the country, much less the world. Max struck me as someone who, in St. Paul's words, wasn't conforming himself to the age but open to transformation. I was thinking maybe I should get Max's app and try it out myself.

The original podcast telling Max's story, however, was followed by a second episode, recorded several months later. And this one com-plicated matters. Apparently sometimes the app—with its design for randomness—was sending users to some profoundly uncomfortable places. One user described a time that Max's app sent her to an event billed as a "midget wrestling strip club," or as she described it in her own words, a "trifecta of exploitation."[10] She wanted to be open to stretching experiences and getting outside of her bubble. She didn't want to be close-minded. At the same time, even being present at such an event evoked a deep discomfort within her. Did attending demon-strate an admirable curiosity about the wider world or did it cross over into the realm of what the Fathers of the Church deride as *curiositas*—a lurid, seedy curiosity? By paying the cover charge to get into the event, was she supporting the ongoing existence of such venues?

Max and his friends were forced to ask, "Are there limits to how much we should be willing to bubble hop?" Are there worlds that we simply should not entertain? Is being neutral and open-minded always the way to go? What should we do about the deep discomfort we sometimes feel? Yes, sometimes it's just because the situation we're in is socially awkward; sometimes it's telling us to be attentive to our safety; but sometimes, might it also be something more? The English writer G. K. Chesterton was known to quip, "An open mind is something like the open mouth, designed to bite down on something solid."[11] Maybe open-mindedness is not really meant to be a permanent stance in life but a step in a bigger journey?

The renewal of mind that St. Paul talks about seems to say so. He doesn't just say to undergo a renewal of mind but to undergo a renewal of mind so that you'll be able to "discern what is the will of God" or, in other words, to discern "what is good and pleasing and perfect." (The will of God and the good are the same thing.)

The renewal of mind that Paul seems to be talking about is what now we might call renewal of conscience—a deeper listening to that voice inside of each of us, nudging us in the direction of what is good and away from what is evil. The voice that says, "Do this. Avoid that." Just like reason is a God-given capacity to help figure out what's real, conscience is a God-given capacity to help figure out what's good. And, like reason, conscience is not just for Christians. Everyone has a conscience. And it's important that we listen to it and not turn it off in the effort of being open-minded. Because while we don't necessarily want to avoid doing things just because they might be awkward, or even just because they make us nervous, we *do* still want to avoid things that aren't good for us or the wider world.

When people ignore the voice of reason, we end up with things such as the Flat Earth Society or climate change denial. When people ignore the voice of conscience, we end up with things such as the Holocaust.

We open our minds not just for the sake of having open minds. We open our minds in order to search for the "good and pleasing and perfect." And we can only do that if we are guided by conscience. So, rather than turn that voice off while on our bubble-bursting adventures, we actually want to pay *more* attention to it. To develop it. To feed it. To nurture it—with the wisdom of the ages, with Church teaching, with sage counsel. (The good news is you don't have to figure everything out all by yourself!) We tend to the conscience so that in whatever random direction the app of life takes us, we only enter an experience, a relationship, an event to the degree that it serves good.

Max's friend says she stood outside the strip club for a while and decided to go in, but she left after only an hour. Indeed, she saw things she'd never seen before, but they were things she knew no one should see. We can't live totally judgment-free lives and simultaneously hope for a more just world. "You have to acknowledge," she said at the end of the podcast, "that sometimes standing up does mean closing off."[12]

Preaching Sample:
WHOSE VOICE AM I MISSING?

TWENTIETH SUNDAY IN ORDINARY TIME YEAR A

SCRIPTURE TEXT: MATTHEW 15:21–28

Then Jesus went from that place and withdrew to the region of Tyre and Sidon. And behold, a Canaanite woman of that district came and called out, "Have pity on me, Lord, Son of David! My daughter is tormented by a demon." But he did not say a word in answer to her. His disciples came and asked him, "Send her away, for she keeps calling out after us." He said in reply, "I was sent only to the lost sheep of the house of Israel." But the woman came and did him homage, saying, "Lord, help me." He said in reply, "It is not right to take the food of the children and throw it to the dogs." She said, "Please, Lord, for even the dogs eat the scraps that fall from the table of their masters." Then Jesus said to her in reply, "O woman, great is your faith! Let it be done for you as you wish." And her daughter was healed from that hour.

One thing we know about Jesus: He had a very strong sense of purpose in his life. He knew who he was and where he wanted to focus his energies. In the passage we read today, he succinctly states his life's mission statement: I am sent "only to the lost sheep of the house of Israel." We can imagine he arrived at that conclusion carefully and gradually through years spent growing up in a Jewish household, studying the scriptures (especially the words of the prophets), and lots and lots of time in prayer. Surely he knew that there were people beyond Israel. But one only has a certain number of years in life. And the people of Israel were his top concern.

The gospel we read today, however, tells us that his conviction was challenged one day as he traveled in the region of Tyre and Sidon, when a Syrophoenician woman begged him to include *her* daughter in his circle of concern.

At first Jesus refuses. It is hard to tell whether he is gently teasing the woman or frankly dismissive, but he refers to her as a "dog"—a derogatory term for non-Jews. The woman doesn't let him off the hook. She rebuts that even dogs are able to eat "scraps that fall from the table of their masters." She makes clear that others beyond his own nation are in need and that the narrowness of his view is limiting the good that could be done.

Then the most amazing thing happens: The Son of God changes his mind. In that moment, Jesus wakes up to the impact that his narrow view of his call is having on others. He gives weight to the woman's voice and expands his circle of concern. In the version of this story that we find in the Gospel of Mark, the impact of the woman's words is even more clear. Jesus doesn't say that it is her faith that heals her daughter but "For saying this, you may go. The demon has gone out of your daughter" (Mk 7:29).

The story became an important one in the Early Church. After Jesus' death and resurrection, the scriptures indicate that the early apostles also struggled with the focus of their preaching mission: Shouldn't they be going out exclusively to the "lost sheep of the house of Israel"? But there were these Gentiles, such as Cornelius, who kept seeking them out. And this overzealous guy named Paul, who was having success all over the Mediterranean basin. And well, maybe, just maybe, we should listen to those persistent voices outside our circle of concern? After all, didn't Jesus do that when the Syrophoenician woman insisted he hear *her* out?

There is a good chance that we non-Jews who are Christian today owe a great debt of gratitude to that plucky Syrophoenician woman and the way her memory functioned in the Early Church. Without her, would the apostles have ever thought global? Would the message of Christ have ever come to us?

All of which seems to indicate that we should give a prized place to the voice of scrappy Syrophoenicians in our own time—people who we think of as outside of our circle of concern, those beyond our immediate families and coworkers who are not part of our daily focus but whose lives are impacted by the choices that we make and who ask us to pay attention to that fact.

We could go global and think about those who remind us that when we vote, we're making a choice that impacts not just our lives but the lives of others halfway around the world who can't vote in our elections. Or we could think about people in our own country whose working conditions or wages are impacted by our seemingly simple choices about where to shop. Or we could think very local, about the man who jingles the can next to our particular entrance to the subway. The point is the same: each of us lives our life with our eyes focused on a particular circle of concern, but the gospel asks us to consider expanding that circle one or two ripples out. To pay attention to the pesky voices of those unwittingly impacted by the convictions we hold. The voices that say, "Hear us out!" The voices that have a crazy faith in our capacity to change our mind and acknowledge their concerns as well.

BUT WHAT ABOUT OTHERS WHO DON'T AGREE WITH US?

Let's say that we are doing our best to inform our conscience and arrive at sound judgments rooted in reality, conscious of the impact our beliefs may have on others. What do we do about the fact that others hold different beliefs than we do, some of which are "differences that make a difference" for us? It's a question on the hearts and minds of many in our communities.

The Church has struggled mightily with this question over the centuries. Historically, the Church has tested a wide range of options in response to others who do not share what the Church holds as true, including everything from praying for the person to arresting them to excommunicating them. In our current pluralistic environment, some of these options no longer make sense (and most of us, I think, would say, "Thank goodness"). Furthermore, such grand solutions as excommunication have never been available to individual Christians in disagreement over such issues as whose turn it is to take out the garbage. There are times when I would like to have all the power of civil and ecclesial law behind me when it comes to solving, once and for all, issues related to living in common with others. But I don't, and so I need other, more practical strategies.

Many of us see communications coaching as outside our job description. Yet if we want people to be able to live truth in their daily lives, that charge inevitably includes being able to talk through differences that make a difference. Helping people overcome differences was certainly a key concern of Jesus' in his proclamation of the kingdom of God, and the scriptures open many doors to reflect on what we've learned as best practices in this regard. What follows are four practices that we can regularly encourage in our preaching, teaching, and leading to equip hearers for handling conversations in which another holds a different truth. These are practices we can also model from the pulpit, in the classroom, and at the conference table, especially when we talk about those who disagree with what the Church holds as true.

Assume Charitable and Reasonable Intent

When we have been careful in the formation of our own opinion and another still thinks differently than we do, our natural impulse is to assume the other is either invincibly ignorant or in the throes of sin. Both of those are possibilities. Ignorance and sin have played a role in human judgment from the earliest pages of Genesis. But the gospel admonition "Stop judging" (Mt 7:1) suggests that in times of difference, we should first assume basic intelligence and good intent on the part of the other. As noted earlier in the preaching sample titled "The Ear of the Wise," in our own head, we may be saying, "The reason why X won't see things my way is that she is flat-out crazy." But in her own head, X is probably not thinking, "The reason I won't change my mind on this matter is because I'm flat-out crazy." In X's head, her opinions somehow make sense, and our first goal is to try to understand why.

Sin and ignorance are possibilities, but it is also possible that X has different data than we do, has selected different data to pay attention to than we have, or is interpreting that selected data differently. Again, as Thomas Aquinas notes, sometimes the difference of perception between us may simply be rooted in the natural messiness of practical reason.

Chances are there is a bit of sin and ignorance intertwined with natural differences in practical reasoning for X, but chances are that it is the case for us as well. Even as intelligent people with good intentions, we still can be unaware of ways in which the filters we use to select and interpret data may be infected with traces of "isms"—racism, sexism, ageism, elitism, and the like. Knowing how much we would like our own possible blind spots to be handled charitably by others, we can lean into conversations assuming the other is a person of intelligence and goodwill who is not consciously intending to do harm.[13] In our effort to model this practice, we should be careful not to malign any group from the pulpit, in the classroom, or in the boardroom, including in the use of labels to describe the group that no one in that group would use to describe themselves or their motivations (e.g., abortionists, the gay agenda, relativists, racists, elites).

Listen at the Lower Rungs of the Ladder

When we want to practice Christian love toward someone who holds convictions different from our own, the most powerful action we can take is to listen. As noted earlier, conversations around differences of opinion tend to start at the top of the ladder of inference. We want to move the conversation to the lower rungs of the ladder by asking questions that will help us understand what lies beneath the other's conclusions:

- "Tell me about what you are seeing that you think I might be missing."
- "What do you think I should be paying more attention to?"
- "This sounds like it is really important to you. Why?"
- "What are you feeling about this experience?"
- "What does this experience mean to you?"
- "What kinds of experiences have you had that shape your thinking on this?"
- "What are you concerned would happen if we went in another direction? What would be lost if we did ___ instead?"[14]

In the end, we still may not agree with their opinion, but we'll understand better why this opinion makes sense for them. We can note that if we had the same experiences, if we were working with the same data, if we were living under the same conditions, we might share similar conclusions. And sometimes that will be enough. As the Benedictine sister Joan Chittister says, "What most people need is a good listening-to."[15] We arrive at a degree of peace, acknowledging that we look at the issue differently but it doesn't need to continue impacting our relationship.

In the pulpit, it is tough to model what good listening looks like. Usually there is one person doing all the talking! Dialogical homilies have their own challenges. But one can easily integrate stories that include snippets of dialogue where the kinds of questions listed are explored. We can paint a picture of what good listening looks like since, sadly, many hearers have not had the experience of receiving a "good listening-to" in their own lives. We can also give evidence in our preaching, teaching, and speaking as leaders of having listened deeply to other perspectives. When mentioning a person or group that sees things differently than you or the Church, describe the other's position in such a way that if a member of the "opposing" party heard you on that day, the person would be able to nod and say, "Yes, that is what I believe. You might not agree with me, but you heard what I said and represented my concern fairly."

Share from the Lower Rungs of Our Ladders

Sometimes . . . well, okay, most of the time . . . we'll find that, even though we now understand the other's perspective better, we are still not okay with agreeing to disagree on the issue. We also have a voice, and it wants to speak. It wants to explain itself, to share why it holds what it holds. It wants to talk about how it is impacted by the other's beliefs. And for the sake of integrity, it is important that our own perspective is shared, even if the other won't change their mind (or even listen!).

Just as we come to deeper understanding of the other by exploring the lower rungs of their ladder, the other has a better chance of understanding us if we speak from the lower rungs of our ladder, and if we do so from a stance of curiosity. Every ladder is complicated, including our own. How our opinions form is a bit of a puzzle, even to ourselves. If we can demonstrate that we are curious before our own ladder, it invites the other to ask more questions of us, and possibly even spurs the other to look at their ladder more carefully. We do this by verbalizing aloud what we wonder about when considering our own ladders: "I realize that _____ might be at stake for me. I'd like to think that I'm not motivated by _____, but sometimes I wonder if I am. When I hear you say that, an alarm bell goes off inside my head. I'm not entirely sure why. I suspect a piece of it is_____. My experience of _____ has shaped my thinking on this. There are probably other experiences that I need to spend more time thinking about."

In chapter 1 we heard Pope Francis say a healthy dose of doubt is important in the pursuit of truth. In parallel fashion, expressing doubt is an important part of exploring what we hold as true. Instead of only sharing the data we have that supports our opinion, we can also share the data we've gleaned that doesn't. We can acknowledge to the other what we think the weak spots in our own arguments might be and what we consider to be the strongest points in their argument. Doing so can quell the urge in others to defend their view because it alerts them that we're already aware of the contrasting data and we're thinking about it. It implicitly invites the other to be transparent about their own doubts, bringing the conversation to a new place where we might discover overlapping concerns.

Again, those of us called to lead can model this kind of reflection in the pulpit, in the classroom, and in the boardroom. For example, when talking about a moral teaching that some hearers might find tough to swallow, after describing charitably the opposing point of view, rather than just share the Church's conclusion, we can describe the original data the Church was working with. What was the Church worried about or concerned might be lost? In what ways does this concern continue? What has been the impact of the teaching on which the Church might continue to reflect?

In the words of Pope Francis, "To dialogue means to believe that the 'other' has something worthwhile to say, and to entertain his or her point of view and perspective. Engaging in dialogue does not mean renouncing our own ideas and traditions, but the claim that they alone are valid or absolute."[16]

Asking for Divine Help

In any conversation worth its salt, we come away having learned something new. Most of the time what we learn will deepen a conviction we already hold. But unless we are already perfectly true in all our judgments, it would seem that at least some of the time, what we learn should be changing our minds.

It's tough to change our mind because we get attached to what we hold as true. As multiple studies document, we humans suffer from "confirmation bias." Once we have reached a particular conclusion, we will pre-sort all future data coming into our ladder based on what it is we already hold—drawing upon agreeable data to reinforce our perspective and dismissing other data as irrelevant.[17]

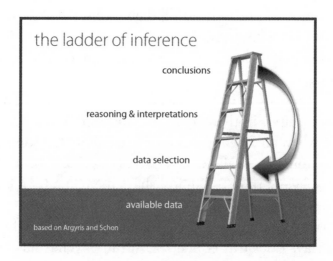

the ladder of inference

conclusions

reasoning & interpretations

data selection

available data

based on Argyris and Schon

As part of a faith tradition that preaches the importance of ongoing conversion, confirmation bias presents a real danger for Christians. We want to be firm in holding on to our convictions, faithful to the wisdom that has been passed on to us. At the same time, we don't want to shut ourselves off from learning something new or lose the ability to change our minds. And so we constantly struggle to find the right balance between conviction and openness.

If anyone figures out exactly what that right balance looks like, alert the pope. Meanwhile, as we try to live that tension rightly, we can practice bringing the struggle to prayer: "God, I don't know how to talk with X anymore. God, help me know whether you want me to be more open here or whether you want me stand firm or whether you want me to live with the ambiguity. God, help the two of us break through this impasse." As noted earlier, God cares a great deal about our ability to communicate with one another, because God wants us to be able to enjoy communion with one another—and those two are deeply linked. These are the kinds of prayers that God delights in answering.

Church leaders can certainly lift up the role of prayer in working through differences and even incorporate examples of prayer into our preaching, teaching, and facilitation. In the preaching sample that follows, I draw attention to one community's deep concern to be able to talk with one of its members. In their effort to bring the matter to Jesus, they model for us what it looks like to bring our concerns around communication to Jesus today.

Preaching Sample:
COMMUNICATION FOR COMMUNION

TWENTY-THIRD SUNDAY IN ORDINARY TIME YEAR B

SCRIPTURE TEXT: MARK 7:31–37

Again [Jesus] left the district of Tyre and went by way of Sidon to the Sea of Galilee, into the district of the Decapolis. And people brought to him a deaf man who had a speech impediment and begged him to lay his hand on him. He took him off by himself away from the crowd. He put his finger into the man's ears and, spitting, touched his tongue; then he looked up to heaven and groaned, and said to him, "*Ephphatha!*" (that is, "Be opened!"). And immediately the man's ears were opened, his speech impediment was removed, and he spoke plainly. He ordered them not to tell anyone. But the more he ordered them not to, the more they proclaimed it. They were exceedingly astonished and they said, "He has done all things well. He makes the deaf hear and [the] mute speak."

For as long as there have been human communities, human communities have struggled with the phenomenon of deafness. Not uncommon among the aging, it is quite uncommon among the young—only about one in every one thousand children is born profoundly deaf. But when it does occur, it often comes with significant challenges.

History testifies that even in ancient times there have been deaf persons who thrived. In the Hittite empire more than 3,500 years ago, a concentration of a particular gene mutation in the population gave birth to a rich deaf culture—a culture still celebrated at places such as Gallaudet University today.

But that should not make us underestimate the challenges faced by children who are deaf, especially when born into hearing communities that are not fluent in the language of signing. It seems that a lot goes on in the brain related to acquiring the structure of language between the ages of eighteen to thirty-six months. If that period is missed, the language centers in a child's brain can atrophy, making it hard to figure out language's mysteries later. Not only is communication affected but also the capacity to grasp abstract thoughts. Even today, only a third of deaf teens graduate from high school. Of those who go on to college, only a fifth complete a degree. Those deaf from childhood can experience profound isolation and increased mental health issues. They are vulnerable in a particular way to sexual abuse.[18]

The man who Jesus encounters in today's gospel appears to be one who experienced deafness from infancy—unable to hear, but also struggling to speak. We don't know the other ways it may have also been impacting his life; we can only guess there were other ways.

I don't think it would be a stretch to say that obviously he was loved by his community; it is the community that brings him to Jesus. But it is also clear that his deafness presents a real challenge for them. They are unable to communicate with one another as they would want. They are asking for healing of what blocks them from being able to participate fully in one another's lives. And we discover that it is a cause Jesus is partial to as well. With his hands and his spit, he opens the man's ears and frees his tongue to speak plainly so that he can be understood.

In today's world, there is an ever-growing number of efforts to mitigate the isolating and limiting side effects of physical deafness, but the challenge of real communication and full participation in a community's life extends far beyond those born into a muted or silent world. The reason that we can so readily empathize with the stories of those who are deaf is that all of us at one time or another have felt as though our modes of communicating with one another are clogged, blocked, or frustratingly muffled.

We all have experiences of seeing lips move but not grasping what is being said. All of us have moments when we are told that we are surrounded by love and concern on all sides, yet we still feel lonely and isolated. All of us can remember times when we've felt as if our tongue refused to serve the longings of our heart. It wouldn't speak the words we wanted it to say. Times when we felt as though we could neither understand nor be understood.

And I suspect that Jesus is still partial to this cause. That Jesus cares a lot about our ability to live lives rich in relationship.

We have often heard that the purpose of our lives is to enjoy "communion." Indeed, every time we gather to celebrate Eucharist, we enact in ritual our belief about where all of history is headed: communion with God and one another. But perhaps we've not thought much before about the fact that communion and communication share the same root. The acts of listening and speaking are meant to make possible deep and abiding *relationship* with one another. Whenever we make an effort to work at the quality of our communication with one another—whenever we open ourselves to listening at a new level, practice care of our words, speak what is most deeply in our hearts— we are, by the very act of doing so, working in service of God's plan for communion.

Long ago, there was a community along the Sea of Galilee near Sidon who so valued being in communion with one another that they sought Jesus' help to make conversation possible where it had seemed impossible. I wonder if in our own communities we go to any such lengths as they did. I wonder if we even think of our ability to be in conversation with one another as intertwined with the spiritual life, a part of what it means to be fully human. I wonder if we even think of the quality of our communication as something Jesus would deeply care about, and something about which we might want to ask his healing help.

As we move into this coming week, the gospel invites us to consider what we might do as a community to grow our capacity to communicate with one another. What would it look like for Christ to work a miracle in *our* midst? What voices would we suddenly be able to hear that we can't right now? What would we want to be freed to say? And what is stopping us now from coming before Jesus and asking for what we need? Nothing. Nothing at all. And so let us bring our prayer before the Lord.

Jesus, we ask you to stand with us now as we call to mind a relationship with another where we feel stuck. We've tried, Lord, to no avail. We've tried listening. We've tried talking. We've tried to be open to changing our minds. We've tried standing up for what we believe. It feels as though we've run out of options. So now we are before you— which is where we probably should have started—asking for you to touch our ears and our mouths and proclaim, "*Ephphatha*." Make possible for us a way forward where there appears to be none. You, Lord, are our hope. Once again, do the miraculous in our midst.

AND WHEN NOTHING WORKS?

It's the question so many of those we serve ask in deep pain. Unfortunately, there are no magic words, no magic techniques for breaking through tough conversations around the truth of one another's beliefs. Occasionally, after giving it our all, even after prayer, we will still find ourselves in a state of impasse. It can be helpful at that point for each party to clarify: "Is there anything that would change your mind on this matter? Is there data that you would find persuasive? What would you have to see in order to change your opinion?" Naming what would persuade us to change our own mind can also give the conversation a potential path forward.

But sometimes not. Sometimes we discover that *no* evidence to the contrary would be sufficient to change another's mind, in which case there may be no purpose to continuing to talk about it. We will discuss whether and how to remain in relationship in chapter 4. But for now, as preachers, teachers, and others who lead within the Church, we should be honest about the human experience of limitation. As much as we might want to bring about a harmony in which all beliefs are held in common, this is ultimately beyond our control. Our planet's future—the kingdom of God of which Jesus speaks—ultimately rests in the hands of God. Even Jesus in his own preaching ministry was unable to change people's minds. Dealing with this realization is part of what it means to live truth as well. In the preaching sample that follows, I highlight Jesus' teaching in this regard.

Preaching Sample:
SHAKE THE DUST
FOURTEENTH SUNDAY IN ORDINARY TIME YEAR C

SCRIPTURE TEXT: LUKE 10:1–12

After this the Lord appointed seventy[-two] others whom he sent ahead of him in pairs to every town and place he intended to visit. He said to them, . . . "Go on your way; behold, I am sending you like lambs among wolves. Carry no money bag, no sack, no sandals; and greet no one along the way. Into whatever house you enter, first say, 'Peace to this household.' If a peaceful person lives there, your peace will rest on him; but if not, it will return to you. Stay in the same house and eat and drink what is offered to you, for the laborer deserves his payment. Do not move about from one house to another. Whatever town you enter and they welcome you, eat what is set before you, cure the sick in it and say to them, 'The kingdom of God is at hand for you.' Whatever town you enter and they do not receive you, go out into the streets and say, 'The dust of your town that clings to our feet, even that we shake off against you.' Yet know this: the kingdom of God is at hand. I tell you, it will be more tolerable for Sodom on that day than for that town."

For the past couple years, I have been doing talks and trainings in various places in the country, working with business and church leaders to develop capacities and skills for working through conversations that they find tough to have. I put a lot of time and energy into this work because I believe in the power of conversation to help people make their way through differences and form deeper relationships with one another. And I can give personal witness to the way that things such as active listening, and separating intention from impact, and looking for common interests when negotiating can change a situation for the better.

But in pretty much every workshop I've ever done—regardless of the background of the participants—there are a couple of people who come up during break to let me know that they've tried all this stuff before with someone in their life—a boss, a government agency, a spouse, a mother-in-law—and it just doesn't work. Things aren't getting any better.

When you are a presenter, it's never a pleasant experience to be told the stuff you are suggesting isn't helpful. And sometimes, I admit, I get suspicious about how much the person has actually tried. But I also have to admit that it *is* possible to try everything in a conversation—to listen well, to try to understand, to look for common interests, et cetera—and the other doesn't respond in kind. It happens. And when I see that sort of weary, drained look in the eyes of the person in front of me, I've come to understand that they are not looking to me for another dazzling communications tip that they've never heard before; they are looking for someone to give them permission to quit trying so hard. Are there times when we can just say, "I give up. This conversation is over"?

It strikes me that today's gospel is immensely practical in this regard. Jesus is sending out seventy-two disciples in pairs to preach about the kingdom of God. They are going to be entering new territory, talking to and staying with people they do not know—presenting to them a way of looking at the world that is totally different from what they would have ever imagined. And he knows some of these towns are going to receive that message and some are going to resist that message. He doesn't tell the disciples to stay indeterminably and slowly drive themselves mad banging their heads against the wall. Instead he gives permission to "shake the dust" and leave things in the hands of God. It's not the disciples' problem to deal with.

Jesus doesn't give a time frame to use as a gauge. How long are they supposed to stick it out before calling it quits? A day? A week? A year? Ten years? This seems to indicate to me that he trusts the disciples' capacity for discernment. That's tricky. Sometimes in my own life, I think I've given up and cut off a conversation too fast. At other times, I think I've probably hung in there for too long when I should have just moved on. It's not easy to tell. When should I listen some more? When should I clarify one more time or try to come up with a better argument? The gospel doesn't offer much help in that regard, but it does give us permission to absent ourselves from situations that don't seem to be going anywhere fruitful.

Interesting to note: We are not to do the other violence because they won't be persuaded by us. We are not to issue threats or dire predictions. We are still expected to speak that "the kingdom of God is at hand," whether they are listening or not. But then we are free to move on. We're not obligated to get a particular outcome.

In your own life, is there a conversation that you are wondering if you have held on to for too long? How will you know when it is time to shake the dust? What would it look like to release it to God's hands?

A SUMMARY OF CHAPTER 2

Living in a post-truth society raises challenging questions for contemporary Christians: Not only "What is truth?" but also "How do I put together all I've learned to form truths—judgments, opinions, conclusions that I hold as true? How do I talk with those who have constructed their data to arrive at different truths?"

Part of announcing the Good News in a contemporary congregation, classroom, or boardroom involves lifting up what we've learned as a faith community over the past two thousand years about how to arrive at truths and also how to assess and continually "improve" our truths—that is, how to make sure our opinions are aligned with the good. An aspect of that work involves highlighting and modeling best practices related to respectful dialogue around truths even in the midst of disagreement. In our preaching, teaching, and leading we want to:

- affirm that, while reality exists and we can know it, our judgments about how best to make sense of reality and live in it are shaped in ways that we don't entirely understand by the various cultures in which we function (family, society, educational systems, faith traditions, etc.);
- affirm that when our judgments impact others, they become moral in nature and must be formed responsibly, which can only happen if we have an ongoing commitment to be grounded in facts; develop our conscience; and weigh the impact of our judgments on others, especially the poor and vulnerable;
- equip hearers with concrete practices for talking with others about differing beliefs, specifically assuming charitable and reasonable intent; listening deeply; speaking reflectively about our own data and interpretations; and praying for divine assistance; and

- acknowledge that we do not ultimately control the outcome of tough conversations around conflicting beliefs and sometimes have to "shake the dust."

Although in the end we may not arrive in a place of agreement, Thomas Aquinas reminds us, "We must love them both, those whose opinions we share and those whose opinions we reject. For both have labored in the search for truth and both have helped us in the finding of it."[19] Whenever we preach about truths that are not all held in common, we want to do so in such a way that it becomes clear: the place of our most profound disagreement with one another is simultaneously the place of opportunity to practice Christian love in a most particular way.

For Reflection and Dialogue

- How aware are you of what lies in the lower rungs of your personal ladder of inference? What influences have most shaped the way that you make sense of the world and arrive at conclusions about how to live in it?
- What struggles do you hear in your community concerning the formation of their opinions and what to do with differing opinions? How have the challenges described in this chapter played a part in the life of your congregation?
- How would you assess the effectiveness of the preaching samples in this chapter in terms of the five markers of effectiveness named in the introduction to this book: having a single message; using a conversational tone; specificity in language; valuing autonomy; and anticipating diversity of perspectives? What do you think would heighten the samples' effectiveness?
- As a preacher or teacher, when is the last time that you tried to address how we arrive at truths or talk about truths? How did it go? What might you try differently the next time around?

- What makes you most nervous about trying to address the formation and discussion of truths in the current climate? How might you be resisting drawing attention to these topics in ministry as a preacher, teacher, or leader? What, if anything, would persuade you to try?
- What connections are you currently seeing between the way that you speak publicly about people who hold different beliefs than the Church and the way your community interacts with those people in their lives?

3.

Truth

AS A WAY OF COMMUNICATING WITH OTHERS

American lore prizes the self-made person but when you think about it, none of us is self-made. We each exist because two people came together before our birth, and that was only the beginning. We commute to school and work on roads paved by others. We cook food harvested by others. We hum tunes composed by others. Whether we like it or not, each of us survives and thrives only as part of a wider network. From a Christian perspective, this arrangement is not happenstance; God intends it. God made us to be in relationship with others. Only by being in relationship with others do we develop the capacities needed to become the people God dreams us to be: a people who can share a life of communion forever with God.

But let's push that basic Christian insight introduced earlier in chapter 2 one step forward and ask, what makes it possible for us to live together in community? What allows us to harness our individual energies around joint projects such as road construction, food production, and music making? *Communication.*

Each of us has a whole jumble of thoughts and feelings, experiences and acquired knowledge inside of ourselves. "Every head is a world," as the proverb goes. But the rich internal life within each person remains a mystery unless it's expressed. Words—spoken, written, or gestured—open the door to what lies inside another. And without words, our efforts to understand one another are often stymied. What parent has not held their crying infant at 2:00 a.m. and moaned, "I just wish you could talk and tell me what's wrong." Words create bridges to worlds otherwise unreachable, and they enable us to do things we could never manage without them.

Our dependency on words is well captured in the ancient tale of Babel found in Genesis 11. The people were trying to build a tower that would be as high as the skies when their capacity to communicate with one another became confused. As a result, they "scattered . . . over all the earth," unable to realize their plan (Gn 11:9). That tower could just as easily have been a school, hospital, television show, or financial institution. *Everything* we construct as a society depends on shared information, which implies an honest relaying of what is going on inside of our heads. If we couldn't do so—or chose not to do so—we wouldn't be able to get anything done together. Imagine trying to build a tower if the engineers couldn't or wouldn't communicate their knowledge of the weight a wall might bear.

The common root shared by the words *community*, *communion*, and *communication* is not coincidental. The Latin *cum* means "with" or "together." From a Catholic perspective, the purpose of communication is to help us build community so that we can experience communion (*CCC* 2469).[1] Sit with the gravity of that statement for a moment. Our ability to live in community—and ultimately that includes our ability to live forever in communion with God—depends on our using words as they were meant to be used: as genuine indicators of what is in our heads.[2]

In chapter 1 we talked about truth as having a mind aligned with reality. In this chapter, we talk about truth as *having one's words aligned with one's mind*. Thomas Aquinas makes a similar distinction when he distinguishes between *veritas* as an objective and veracity as a virtue that should be evident in all our words and actions.[3] The two are related but not synonymous. It is possible to have a mind that accurately grasps reality but that doesn't share that information or shares it inaccurately. It is also possible to be sincere and speak transparently about what's on your mind while what your mind thinks is real is not actually real.

If your mind is aligned with reality and you say something you know not to be real, that qualifies as a lie. If you are sincere but not connected with what's real—perhaps because you are ill informed or you missed a step when thinking something through or, in some cases, suffering from a mental illness—that qualifies as an error. Sometimes as a listener it is hard to tell the difference: "Is this person lying to me? Or do they believe what they are saying, though it seems off-base to me?" Both challenge a community's ability to function well.

Because so much depends on truthfulness in communication, everyone should be concerned about the issue—preachers and teachers in particular. The ministry of the Word that we pour our lives into is entirely dependent on taking words seriously—a point that I emphasize in the preaching sample that follows. When emphasizing the importance of truthfulness in the current context, the message may be critiqued as political (a topic we will return to later), but truthfulness is a fundamental faith issue. Christianity, too, stakes its survival on the ability of words to communicate. We cannot avoid the topic for fear of ruffling feathers. The preaching sample that follows attempts to raise awareness of how critical truthfulness is for every aspect of our lives, including our faith lives.

Preaching Sample:
BLESSED ARE THOSE WHO HAVE NOT SEEN
SECOND SUNDAY OF EASTER
SCRIPTURE TEXT: JOHN 20:24–31

> Thomas, called Didymus, one of the Twelve, was not with them when Jesus came. So the other disciples said to him, "We have seen the Lord." But he said to them, "Unless I see the mark of the nails in his hands and put my finger into the nailmarks and put my hand into his side, I will not believe." Now a week later his disciples were again inside and Thomas was with them. Jesus came, although the doors were locked, and stood in their midst and said, "Peace be with you." Then he said to Thomas, "Put your finger here and see my hands, and bring your hand and put it into my side, and do not be unbelieving, but believe." Thomas answered and said to him, "My Lord and my God!" Jesus said to him, "Have you come to believe because you have seen me? Blessed are those who have not seen and have believed."

Since we've heard the proclamation of Jesus' resurrection last Sunday, the gospel readings of this past week have taken us on a strange ride. Left and right, Jesus keeps appearing to friends who, once they've "seen the Lord," go and tell Jesus' other friends what they've seen . . . and no one believes them . . . until *those* friends have an experience in which they "see" and share . . . and find no one believes *them.*

We could say that this pattern climaxes in today's gospel passage with Thomas, who apparently has taken the slow boat from China to the unfolding drama of the week. Like the others before him, he refuses to believe based only on the witness of others; he needs to see for himself. And once he sees, he is entirely bowled over.

Two things seem obvious here: (1) seeing the risen Lord is clearly a very powerful and persuasive experience, and (2) hearing about the risen Lord from others clearly is not.

That presents a bit of a problem for Jesus, doesn't it? Because once he ascends, the witness of those remaining is the only way that news of the Resurrection is going to be passed on. Future generations won't get to see him and cling to his feet and eat breakfast with him on the seashore and touch the nail marks in his hands. And Jesus knows this will be much harder. How much more fragile a system of belief that comes through the ear rather than through the eye!

What makes believing by the ear rather than the eye so much trickier? Well, it's entirely based on trust that what someone else is saying is true. And sometimes, let's admit it, our words have flowed loose and free. Sometimes we've told tall tales. We've exaggerated. We've protected ourselves by telling flat-out lies. And each time we've done that, we've made it just a little bit harder for those around us to believe what we say in the future—and not just to believe *us* but to believe words in general.

Moreover, sometimes we've been lied to. Others have exaggerated with us. They've made up stuff and we fell for it. Because of that, we have a hard time trusting. Rightly so. Indeed, we have such a hard time trusting that even when other people are doing their best to tell us the truth of what they've experienced, if it doesn't match our own experience, we refuse to listen. We can think here of children who tried to tell us about sexual abuse in the Church; of women who tried to tell us about sexual harassment in the workplace; of African Americans who tried to tell us about their experiences of police violence; of rural communities who tried to tell us about what opioids were doing to their towns. There's a lot that is hard to believe when we've become jaded.

Yet it is to the weak and fragile world of the spoken word that the gospel of the death and resurrection of Jesus Christ is nevertheless entrusted. As Jesus says at the end of today's passage, "Blessed are those who have not seen and have believed." Of course, he's talking about us here. Because unlike Mary Magdalene, Peter, Thomas, Cleopas, or any of those first disciples, we haven't "seen the Lord." The faith we have is a gift that has come to us through our ears. It's come because someone came into our life who was a trustworthy witness and because we were willing to listen long enough that we came to realize that what they were saying was true.

But the fact that this path to faith has stood the test of time for two thousand years does not mean that it is not still fragile. Its continuance depends entirely on the continuance of witnesses who speak only words that can be trusted and on the openness of hearers who are willing to listen deeply to words that at first don't seem to make a whole lot of sense. Every lie that gets told, every bit of fake news passed on, every exaggeration that makes a mountain out of a molehill ... it all chips away at the foundation of trust that our Christian faith depends upon. It makes it harder for sincere witnesses and harder for sincere listeners.

This coming week, in honor of the Easter season, how fitting it would be for each of us to do a check on our own use of words—speaking and listening with great care to one another so that the Good

News of the risen Christ might yet find safe passage in our generation. Blessed are we who have not seen and still believe.

ARE WE SUPPOSED TO SAY EVERYTHING THAT IS ON OUR MINDS?

How many times have you heard someone say something very harsh, followed by the justification, "Well, I'm just being honest!"? Practicing truthfulness as a virtue implies far more than doing a download of every assorted thought in our heads. Truthfulness means being careful that everything that comes out of our mouths is aligned with what is actually in our heads, but it does not mean everything that is in our heads needs to come out of our mouths.

Thomas Aquinas acknowledges that any virtue taken to an extreme becomes a vice. In his writing about truthfulness, he notes the danger of saying too much.[4] There are times when our words may be true but they serve the purpose of making *us* look good or smart rather than building up community. In my own life, I can think of times when I've become very excited about an idea that strikes me in the middle of a conversation but it sidetracks the conversation and doesn't help the group do its work. Worse, I can think of instances when I've shared what someone else said to me in confidence.

But Aquinas also notes the danger of saying too little.[5] Maybe because of low self-esteem or false humility; maybe because we want to hold information for our own benefit; maybe out of fear of repercussion, we don't share what we know, even when it would be beneficial to others that we do so. I think of times when I've spotted a potential flaw in a plan but didn't bring it up because I didn't want to look foolish if I was wrong. Or I recall times I've been party to decisions that made me morally uncomfortable, but I didn't want to rock the boat and so remained silent.

Truthfulness lies between these extremes, yet the path is not always clear. One person's willingness to share their previous personal experience may come across as TMI (too much information) to some, whereas another's sense of appropriateness could be interpreted by others as unwillingness to engage. Aquinas helps us think through this tension by setting his comments about truthfulness within his larger chapter on justice. Justice, as he describes it, is the constant effort to give each person in the community what they are due.[6] In his mind, truthfulness fits under the category of justice because it is giving each person *the information* that they are due.[7] Judges, for example, have a right to the information needed to make good, well-informed judgments. Health-care proxies have a right to the information needed to make wise decisions around end-of-life care.

When thinking in these terms, whether we should share information in a given situation sometimes becomes clearer: Does the person need this information in order to do their job well? In order to make a good decision? In order to do what society has entrusted them to do? If so, yes, we should share the information we have in our heads. But giving a person only the information that they have a right to seems a low bar in relationships that we value. Strong work collaborations, friendships, and marriages deepen only when there is a spirit of generosity—a willingness to give more to the other than what the other might claim as a right. That includes more information. How do we know how much to say in these situations?

Many of us would acknowledge that even in the relationships we care about most there exists a sizable gap between what we really think and feel and what we will say aloud. Gaps are understandable. We all have experiences of times when we shared what was in our heads and it didn't go well. We spoke with sincerity and were made fun of. We shared an opinion and another critiqued it or was offended. We were honest about how we felt and it ended a friendship. In these situations, trying to be truthful with our words didn't build up our relationships; it hurt them. And so, as human beings who have acquired a few bumps and bruises along the way, gaps make sense. The problem is that gaps can be dangerous to relationships as well. Relationships in which thoughts and feelings are not regularly shared over time drift toward shallow waters. For some relationships that might be fine. We may not care to get any closer to our letter carrier or pharmacist. But for relationships we value? Gaps can cause marriages to atrophy, friendships to fizzle. We start scanning for new job postings in our field.

Part of the reason relationships struggle when there is a large gap between what we think or feel and what we say is because our actions continue to be shaped by what lies in our heads whether we want them to or not. Just because I don't tell you when I'm angry doesn't mean that you can't tell something is wrong. It only gives you less understanding as to why. Truthful communication is to relationships what food is to the body. It is what nourishes relationships, gives them heft, and makes them grow.

All of which is to say that living truth in our communication with others is rarely a straightforward affair. Even in our closest relationships—perhaps especially in our closest relationships—we constantly need to discern how much to share and how much to keep to ourselves. Just as getting a good picture of reality is tricky, and just as adjudicating judgments is tricky, figuring out what holy honesty looks like in any given situation or relationship is—surprise, surprise—tricky. How much to say remains a matter of judgment. (See how the various dimensions of living truth are so intricately intertwined!)

Aquinas simply cautions that whatever information we share needs to be shared charitably—in essence, lovingly. What we deem important for the other person to know may not be what the other person wants to hear—for example, "The results of the feedback survey were not favorable" or "It really peeves me that you didn't manage to pick up the kids on time." But the information can still be shared with concern for the person and their dignity.[8] Aquinas is, of course, not alone in this conviction. Many other thinkers, Christian and otherwise, have noted the importance of kindness in our words. We'll sometimes hear the points raised here summarized as three questions we should ask ourselves before speaking: Is it true? Is it necessary? Is it kind?[9] I suspect Aquinas would agree those are the questions we should be asking, but he would want to add a bit of nuance:

- Is what I am about to say rooted in reality as best as I can tell?
- Is what I am about to say helpful? Are they owed this information in justice? Does the relationship call for more?
- If so, how will I say it with love?

Knowing that we are guiding our congregations through complicated terrain, one of the more helpful things that we can do is lift up models of what it looks like to lovingly speak about what's in one's head, as well as models of what it looks like to lovingly hold back information. In the two preaching samples that follow, I offer an example of both. In "The Day After," I create a dialogue between Jesus and the mother of James and John to model what a tough honest conversation might look like when both parties have much in their heads that they deem true and necessary for the other to hear, even if the other may not want to hear it. Although the conversation is messy and not "nice," I do think that it models loving speech. In "All That He Didn't Say," I imagine what is in Timothy's head when he receives one of Paul's letters. From Timothy's perspective, the information he could share is true, but at least for the time being Timothy decides not to write Paul his thoughts. Knowing that Paul is going through a hard time, he recognizes that for Paul to hear all this would probably not be helpful. He chooses to respond with a loving act. He can speak another day.

Preaching Sample:
THE DAY AFTER
SCRIPTURE TEXT:
MATTHEW 20:20–28

Then the mother of the sons of Zebedee approached [Jesus] with her sons and did him homage, wishing to ask him for something. He said to her, "What do you wish?" She answered him, "Command that these two sons of mine sit, one at your right and the other at your left, in your kingdom." Jesus said in reply, "You do not know what you are asking. Can you drink the cup that I am going to drink?" They said to him, "We can." He replied, "My cup you will indeed drink, but to sit at my right and at my left, [this] is not mine to give but is for those for whom it has been prepared by my Father." When the ten heard this, they became indignant at the two brothers. But Jesus summoned them and said, "You know that the rulers of the Gentiles lord it over them, and the great ones make their authority over them felt. But it shall not be so among you. Rather, whoever wishes to be great among you shall be your servant; whoever wishes to be the first among you shall be your slave. Just so, the Son of Man did not come to be served but to serve and to give his life as a ransom for many."

I came upon her the morning after along the riverbank, beating the last remnants of dirt and color out of a thin piece of cloth with a rock and then rinsing them down stream. I'd heard from Mark that her name was Salome, but I did not dare address her by her given name, for she was a very traditional woman wedded to Zebedee and to the culture of her time, so she didn't really have a name and thought that *appropriate*.

When I spotted her, even from a distance, I knew I'd seen her before . . . No, maybe she just looked like someone else I knew. Well, you know, come to think of it, she kinda looked like Mary of Nazareth. Maybe the old apocrypha really was true and they *were* sisters. If so, it would make a little more sense as to why she'd been so brazen yesterday: going up to Jesus like that and asking that *her* two sons—and hers only—be seated at Jesus' right and left hands in the kingdom. If they were related, well, then it would only be *appropriate*.

It wasn't that she didn't want to see real changes. Oh no, she did. You could hear it in the cracking of one rock against another and the vigor with which she wrung excess water from the twisted garment. Like all of her neighbors, she despised the Romans. She despised the corruption in her own people's leaders—the extortion and wastefulness more befitting foreign rulers than those set apart to be a light to the nations. She was one who had waited in sincere hope for the coming of the Messiah who would set her people free, while so many of the religious leaders in Jerusalem only gave the aspiration lip service.

And Jesus . . . Jesus had that magnetic charisma, that born-leader quality that could make change happen. Hadn't she been one of the first to spot it? Hadn't she been one to encourage him to dream big dreams since his childhood? When others had scoffed—"What good could come from Nazareth? Really, a carpenter's son?"—hadn't she defended him before the naysayers? Hadn't she encouraged her sons to go with him, even if it meant she and Zebedee were left alone for long periods of time in their old age? Was it really too much to ask that her Jimmy and her Johnny get key positions in his coming administration? Isn't it only *appropriate* that those roles should go to the people who have been with him from the very beginning?

But things had not gone the way she'd planned. No, not at all. She'd waited for what she thought was just the right moment to make the ask, but then, instead of a simple yes, Jesus answered. . . . Well, he didn't answer *her*, that's for sure. It was like she wasn't even there, and all hell broke loose. Her sons were shamed and Jesus' band of men all started arguing with one another. And she . . . she slunk away without anyone noticing, and now even her sons weren't talking to her. "Woman," their eyes seemed to say, "what'd you go and do that for?"

After a while, she threw the garment into a bucket and sat back on her haunches, elbows resting on knees, staring into the river. I was afraid she might turn around and see me, and if that happened I wouldn't be quite sure what to say. So I was considering slinking off myself when I noticed that Jesus was drawing near and squatting down alongside her.

"Auntie," he said.

She rose to her full height of five feet two and turned to look down on him, her eyes flashing with anger and hurt: "I don't understand you. We have been without any say over our lives for so long. You could change that. You could make things different for us if you were in charge."

"Auntie," he said again, "you want to work the system. I want to crack the system. You want to keep the game and just change the players at the top. I want to rewrite the rules of the game."

"Well, what's stopping you? I'm waiting. I've been waiting for a long time for this world to be different."

"Well, certainly the guys over there are not the quickest of learners, as I needed to explain to them again yesterday. But quite frankly, Auntie, one of the things that is also making it difficult is people like you," he said.

"Me!" she exclaimed with outrage. "Me! I am an old woman who has worked hard my whole life and have not a shekel to show for it. I am entirely dependent on my husband and two grown sons to take care of me, and those sons are currently unemployed, apparently with dim future prospects. How can *I* be the problem? *I* don't even own a name."

"My point precisely. The system is stacked against you, but it only works if you agree to keep it working."

"And *how*, pray tell, do *I* agree to keep it working?"

"By assenting to the fact that power is to be feared and that others get to call the shots. By agreeing that titles mean something and treating people differently when they have one. By assuming that when you are told to go along with something, the only possible response is 'Okay.' By not asking questions when you see something you think is unfair. By sulking away and swallowing your anger and hurt rather than speaking it aloud. By not demanding that you have your own name. By limiting your thinking and your actions to what society considers *appropriate*. When you do these things—whether you mean to or not—you are keeping the system alive and well."

"But not to do so is very dangerous. I want to survive."

"Well, now we arrive at the truth. I, honestly, would rather die than do those things."

"Don't say it, Jesus. Don't . . ."

Only at this point did he stand up. "Auntie, do not worry. I will show you how it is done."

There was a long pause.

"So, who really *is* going to sit on your right and your left?" she asked.

"You're asking the wrong question," he said.

"So you've made clear, but I'm just curious."

"A tiny Albanian woman in a sari and a crazy beggar from the mountains of Italy."

"Oh, okay," she said, looking confused.

I wondered if she would stay with him now that her hopes had been dashed, her game board ripped in two. I wondered if maybe she might just leave James and John to their own fates and retire to the comfort of Zebedee's protection for her remaining days. But as Jesus walked away, something of a smile crossed her face, even as a tear rolled down from the corner of her eye.

And *then* I remembered where I'd seen her before. At the tomb, on the third day. *She* was one of those Easter-morning women with courage strong enough to go out in the deep darkness before dawn armed only with spices. Strong enough to confront soldiers and rocks three times her size.

Preaching Sample:
ALL THAT HE DIDN'T SAY
FEAST OF ST. LUKE THE EVANGELIST
SCRIPTURE TEXT:
2 TIMOTHY 4:10–17B

For Demas, enamored of the present world, deserted me and went to Thessalonica, Crescens to Galatia, and Titus to Dalmatia. Luke is the only one with me. Get Mark and bring him with you, for he is helpful to me in the ministry. I have sent Tychicus to Ephesus. When you come, bring the cloak I left with Carpus in Troas, the papyrus rolls, and especially the parchments.

> Alexander the coppersmith did me a great deal of harm;
> the Lord will repay him according to his deeds. You too be on
> guard against him, for he has strongly resisted our preaching.
> At my first defense no one appeared on my behalf, but
> everyone deserted me. May it not be held against them!
> But the Lord stood by me and gave me strength, so that
> through me the proclamation might be completed and all
> the Gentiles might hear it.

Timothy wiped his hands on the front of his robe and opened the scroll with the eager curiosity of a student receiving back a major paper. He speed-read through the entirety of Paul's letter, obviously anxious to see what was at the end. I knew that later he'd go back and savor all the earlier paragraphs, but right now he needed to know how this all turned out.

"Mmmhmmm. Mmmhmmm. Huh. Gotcha." He mumbled along the way as his eyes scanned downward. But as he got to the end, his face puckered. He sighed and sat down, the fully unrolled scroll spilling off his lap onto the floor.

"Well," he finally said, "at least he's still got Luke."

"What happened to all the others? Where's he at? What's going on?" I exclaimed.

"Well, it's the same old story. He's managed to get himself arrested—again—and he's burned almost all his bridges. Demas has left the picture. Crescens and Titus are gone. Can't tell whether they left on their own accord or whether Paul told them to go somewhere. Knowing Paul, probably to Hades. No one was at his first hearing.

"Now he wants me to come and bring Mark with me. Yeah, that's gonna go well. Only a couple of years ago he was accusing Mark of abandoning him. Last time Barnabas mentioned bringing Mark back on a mission, the old man got so bent out of shape that he ended up breaking off his friendship with Barnabas as well. But now he wants me and Mark to bring him his cloak and parchments—traveling from Ephesus to Rome because he needs a coat before winter. Unbelievable."

"Yeah," I sympathized. "That's like a month's journey, even in good weather." I could tell a part of him just wanted to take the scroll and toss it in the fire. "You seem irritated," I said.

"Who wouldn't be?" he countered. "Paul can be so clueless. All of the time he's getting into arguments with everyone who tries to work with him. And he's always sure that he's right. He's always sure that he's the victim in the situation, that the Lord is on his side. When I was younger it was easier to put up with; I so looked up to him. He's a very charismatic person. My mom and grandma adore him. But you have no idea how hard it is to travel with him. He has little patience for any view other than his own."

"But Luke is still with him?"

"Luke is still hanging in there," he confirmed.

"That's interesting," I commented.

"Luke's a saint," Timothy explained. "He's a better man than Demas, Mark, Barnabas, Alexander the coppersmith, and me combined."

"What makes him different?" I asked.

"Well, Luke is slow and steady . . . like an ox. Maybe it's his medical training or something. He knows how to stay calm when someone is injured."

"What about if they are injured in their heart?" I asked.

"Same. He just listens," Timothy replied. "Doesn't agree with'ya or disagree with'ya, just listens. He's patient, even if you're saying the same thing for the twelfth time in a row. He forgives your quirks. He looks for the best in you. Knows your intentions could still have been good, even when it all turned out wrong. He just loves you as you are."

He went on: "You know, Luke is always remembering stories of Jesus that the rest of us barely recall. Like the parable of the unlikely Samaritan who got out his first aid kit to help the wounded man on the side of the road. Or the parable of the father who forgave his bedraggled son who had done him so much harm. I think Luke just has a special place in his heart for the wounded in any form they come."

"Sounds like Paul is a bit wounded right now," I remarked.

"Yes," said Timothy, "he's getting older, he feels all alone. He still has a hundred ideas and trips in his head. He gets mad about *this* person blocking his way and *that* person telling him no. I think he feels as if he's running out of time. But when Paul starts ranting and panicking, Luke doesn't get himself all triggered by Paul being Paul. Luke just remains Luke."

"All of us should be so lucky to have a friend like that," I said.

"Yet what a challenge to be a friend like that," Timothy said, as he stared off into space. And for a minute I did, too, thinking of someone I love and admire, who I can also find maddening to the nth degree.

"Maybe you should tell Luke to write down his stories so that we can keep them always before us when we are exasperated by those we work with and live with and travel with . . . and love."

"I'll mention that when I see him next," Timothy nodded.

"When will that be?" I asked.

"Well, I guess that depends on when the next boat for Rome leaves. You'll excuse me. I guess I need to go track down Mark and find that accursed cloak. My mother will know where the parchments are." He sighed again, but stood, quickly rolling up Paul's letter. So, I stood as well.

"Courage, my soul!" I saluted.

And then we turned from each other and parted ways. Each of us had wounded, old friends out there waiting to be loved again exactly as they are.

Is It Ever Okay to Lie?

We've said that truthfulness is an alignment of our words with what is actually in our heads, but that not everything in our heads needs to be spoken in order to be truthful. For any number of reasons—simple kindness, respect for confidentiality, the realization that we are currently too angry to choose the right words—we can and should keep certain thoughts to ourselves. But is it ever okay to lie?

Lying is different than withholding some of what is in our heads. Lying is saying words that we don't actually believe to be true. So as to let actors off the hook, many philosophers, including Aquinas, add "with the intent to deceive."[10] If you are standing on stage belting out, "I am I, Don Quixote, the Lord of La Mancha," even though you know you are not the Lord of La Mancha, it is not a lie because it is not your intent to deceive the theater audience. They also know that what you are claiming is not meant to be taken as true.

What's thornier is whether it's ever okay to say something you don't believe to be true *with* the intent to deceive—in essence, with the intent that the other person would take it to be true. When philosophers ponder this question, they often do so with extreme scenarios. For example, if a Nazi soldier came to your door and asked if you had any Jews hiding in your attic, and you do, must you say yes? But we could ask the same question regarding everyday scenarios: Is it okay to tell children there is a tooth fairy? Is it okay to tell a friend they look smashing in an outfit when you think anything but?

Some philosophers, such as the eighteenth-century German Immanuel Kant, would say that lying is always wrong.[11] He would argue that, since communities can only function if there is a presumption of honesty in communication, truthfulness is a "duty that must be regarded as the basis of all duties" and must be practiced at all times and everywhere.[12] Others make decisions in their lives based on what we tell them. If, in fact, we tell them something we know to be untrue, we are in some way manipulating their decisions—an action that is fundamentally disrespectful to a fellow human being.

Others would disagree, noting that lying considered in isolation is wrong, but life's moments don't happen in isolation. The decisions that we make around lying take place within complicated circumstances in which there may be multiple wrongs to consider. In the case of the Nazi at the door, it is wrong to lie, but it is also wrong to do something that you know will cause another harm. Sometimes the best we can do in a situation is to choose the lesser of two wrongs.[13] This position doesn't deny that lying in general is wrong, but it acknowledges there are circumstances where it is justifiable.

The problem is that once we acknowledge that lying may be justifiable in certain circumstances, we tend to use this argument a lot—not only to save people's lives from imminent death but also to avoid noxious meetings ("Oh, I'm so sorry. I totally forgot!") and add spice to the holidays ("Yes, and he has a sled pulled by reindeer!"). There are moral goods to be had in these situations, but it would be worth asking whether in the long run they supersede the good of truthfulness.

Sometimes we'll hear it said that lying is okay as long as there is no harm done, but harm is difficult to measure and not always immediate. Every time we engage in even a "white lie," we chip away at the cornerstone that society itself is built upon. So unless we want the whole "tower" to crumble, it makes sense that we take our chisel to it as little as possible. And perhaps especially so with children, who are forming patterns of communicating that will influence the rest of their lives. As a friend once asked me concerning Santa Claus, "Why would you, as a parent who is trying to raise her child in the faith, want to tell your child that there is an invisible figure who brings good things to good children? A figure they will later find out does not exist." If we want our children to trust our words in the future, we probably want to make sure we only tell them things we ourselves believe.

Setting aside complicated philosophical debates about Nazis and white lies for a moment, as Christian leaders we need to acknowledge that scripture repeatedly condemns lying.[14] And whereas the oft-cited eighth commandment of the Decalogue only specifically refers to perjury (lying under oath in a court of law), the *Catechism of the Catholic Church* understands the commandment to cover a wide array of "offenses against the truth" (*CCC* 2464), including lying more broadly, calling it "the most direct offense against the truth" which "by its very nature . . . is to be condemned" (*CCC* 2483, 2485). So while we may or may not wish to address the question of Nazis or Santa Claus from the pulpit (even I concede that one!), we should not avoid preaching, teaching, and talking about lying as a sin. Our faith demands speaking it.

In a post-truth society, preaching about lying is a dicey affair. Condemning lying, like extoling truthfulness, is now also considered "getting political in the pulpit." Granted, to say that a preaching is political is not necessarily a bad thing. Politics, simply defined, is the art of working out how to live with one another. In that sense, much of the Bible has to do with politics, and therefore we can't evade political preaching. When people critique preaching as political, however, they don't generally seem to be concerned that the preacher is talking on the art of relationship. Their worry is that the preaching is targeting or favoring one political figure or issue currently in the news. The preacher is taking sides. The pulpit is never the place to make *ad hominem* attacks (as if there were any such place), but the scriptures themselves take sides on issues. To avoid talking about what the Word of God has to say on issues when they are present both in the text and on the front page of the newspaper constitutes negligence on the part of the preacher. Lying is one of the issues scripture itself takes sides on.

I cannot remember the last time I heard preaching on the sin of lying. Granted, preaching about sin is never easy, but our collective silence on one of the most significant hindrances to living truth is puzzling and problematic. We live in a society that is growing increasingly accustomed to lies—accommodating them rather than challenging them—and it seems that we who are called to Church leadership are in danger of following suit. In the preaching sample that follows, I attempt to directly confront lying as a sin. I am not sure that I got the tone right. In preaching on this topic, I was trying to avoid condemnation of the person while being clear about the condemnation of lying. Perhaps in your own reflections and conversations you will surface better ways of talking straightforwardly on the topic.

Preaching Sample:
PRAYING FOR AN EMBER

FIFTH SUNDAY OF ORDINARY TIME, YEAR C

SCRIPTURE TEXT: ISAIAH 6:1–8

In the year King Uzziah died, I saw the Lord seated on a high and lofty throne, with the train of his garment filling the temple. Seraphim were stationed above; each of them had six wings: with two they covered their faces, with two they covered their feet, and with two they hovered. One cried out to the other:

> "Holy, holy, holy is the LORD of hosts!
>   All the earth is filled with his glory!"

At the sound of that cry, the frame of the door shook and the house was filled with smoke.

Then I said, "Woe is me, I am doomed! For I am a man of unclean lips, living among a people of unclean lips, and my eyes have seen the King, the LORD of hosts!" Then one of the seraphim flew to me, holding an ember which he had taken with tongs from the altar.

He touched my mouth with it. "See," he said, "now that this has touched your lips, your wickedness is removed, your sin purged."

Then I heard the voice of the Lord saying, "Whom shall I send? Who will go for us?" "Here I am," I said, "send me!"

At the close of 2018, Glenn Kessler, the fact-checker at the *Washington Post*, reported that the US president had publicly spoken his 7,645th lie since taking office. That's 7,645 lies in 710 days, or an average of 10.8 lies per day. Kessler has not been counting the number of times the president expresses an opinion. Differences of opinion are a part of everyone's life, especially in politics, and would be impossible to count. Kessler's task has been to go through recorded statements of the president and identify statements that are factually untrue or misleading and able to be proven so—the kinds of things that involve numbers and hard data, such as how many people died in Hurricane Maria or whether an event happened on a given date or not.

From the perspective of Catholic moral theology, let me be the first to admit that some of these technically may not have been lies. They may have been errors. Mistakes. The president may not have intended to share false information. None of us knows what is going on inside of the president's mind and whether he is what in moral theology we call "culpable" for passing on misinformation. None of us knows the state of his soul before God. But as we tie ourselves in pretzels to make sure that we have added the appropriate number of caveats, is it still okay to say the word *lie* from the pulpit? And if not now, then when? Have we become so jittery about the term that we are hesitant to acknowledge that there *is* such a thing anymore? And that God considers it a sin?

How inconvenient this moment in history is for those of us who don't really care to offer or listen to preaching about sin, especially when it hits so close to home. How much easier it would be to look away and talk about something else. But then in our prayer with the scriptures, we find ourselves meditating on passages such as those of Proverbs: "Truthful lips endure forever, the lying tongue, for only a moment. . . . Lying lips are an abomination to the LORD, but those who are truthful, his delight" (Prv 12:19, 22). In our study of the catechism, we are reminded, "Lying is the most direct offense against the truth. To lie is to speak or act against the truth in order to lead someone into error. By injuring man's relation to truth and to his neighbor, a lie offends against the fundamental relation of man and of his word to the Lord" (*CCC* 2483). Lying is not an issue on which we are supposed to remain neutral. And my fear is that *not* to talk about what is on the front page of our newspapers implies a certain kind of consent—that we are okay with the 7,645 lies, that this is the new normal, that we shouldn't expect anything different. But deep down, we know. We know that, regardless of our personal political leanings, it is not sup-posed to be this way.

I'm not sure entirely why we are so hesitant to name what is going on. Perhaps we feel powerless to do anything about it. Perhaps we're not sure how to express our deep discomfort in a way that can be heard. Perhaps we think there are more important things to worry about than lying. But perhaps it is because we know how easy it is to lie. How many things slip from our lips before we've hardly thought about it? Meant to protect ourselves? Make ourselves look good? Skirt a problem?

It is interesting that when Isaiah first received his call to be a prophet, his first response was, "Woe is me, I am doomed! For I am a man of unclean lips, living among a people of unclean lips" (Is 6:5). He knew that he belonged to a culture filled with lies. He knew that it was a problem in the eyes of God—an abomination, if you will. And he knew that he was every bit a part of the problem. But what is beautiful about the story of Isaiah's call is that God has a fix for that. Now, granted, it is a rather unusual fix: one of God's seraphim takes up a set of tongs and sterilizes Isaiah's lips by holding a burning ember to them. "Ouch!" we might think. But God has freed Isaiah's lips to do what lips are meant to do: speak truthful things.

And, oh, the things Isaiah's lips said! The evils of his own time that he so clearly denounced. The Good News he so vividly announced. The promises that the human race's hopes have hung upon now for 2,500 years and counting. Even to this day, we cling to Isaiah's words, especially every Advent and Lent, but even now in Ordinary Time.

We can't control what other people do with their lips. But we can be clear about what we want to do with ours. And there is nothing stopping us here and now from asking God to purify our lips—to forgive whatever lies we have spoken, to singe away any inclination to lie again, to free our mouth to speak only things that are true. Praying this way is a dangerous activity. If God grants what we ask, we should know that this may well impel *us* to denounce evil—including instances of lying in our world today. It could—as in Isaiah's case—also impel us to speak out more about what is good and holy, where God is in our midst, making impossible things possible. People may look at us strange. If you're not okay with these risks, it's probably better not to pray. But if you have the courage to admit that you're a person of unclean lips living among a people of unclean lips, and you are open to God doing something about that, I invite you to bow your head with me now in prayer. Say to God in the silence of your heart whatever it is that you have to say and open yourself to whatever God wants to do in you—whatever God wants to do with your lips.

CAN WE LIE BY OUR ACTIONS?

In this chapter we've been talking about living truth by aligning the words we use to express ourselves with what is in our minds. But there is another way that we express our inner selves, and that is by our deeds. Aquinas recognized that there often exists a mismatch between these two types of expression. We paint a picture of the type of person we are with our words, but our actions reveal something different.[15] This particular variance on lying is often referred to as hypocrisy, coming from the Greek word *hypokrites*, referring to a masked stage actor pretending to be someone they are not.

Hypocrisy irked Jesus in a way few other things did, sometimes driving him to hyperbole. He likened hypocrites to "whitewashed tombs, which appear beautiful on the outside, but inside are full of dead men's bones and every kind of filth" (Mt 23:27). He noted they were blind to their own faults even as they nitpicked on others (Lk 6:42). Indeed, some scripture scholars think that Jesus' mysterious condemnation of "blasphemes against the holy Spirit" as the only unforgivable sin (Mk 3:29) was probably meant as a condemnation of hypocrisy: a person can become so confused about who they actually are in the midst of all the deceit that they no longer think they need forgiveness.[16]

Hypocrisy also seems to irk contemporary hearers in a way few other things do. As examples of hypocrisy in political and ecclesial life create headlines, surveys and interviews conducted for the 2018 Bishops' Synod on Youth highlight the concern young adults in particular have for institutional integrity and personal authenticity.[17] Surely a primary request of the faithful is that their preachers, teachers, and other leaders be persons of integrity and authenticity themselves. They want to know that we believe what we say and do our best to align our words and our actions in our own lives. But they also have a heightened interest in hearing us speak about integrity and authenticity as a path of life. If we want to stir interest in truth as a whole way of life, I suspect that preaching about authenticity and integrity—more than mention of relativism, reason, or even honesty—provides the best entry point for introducing the broader topic. In the preaching that follows, I give an example of what preaching on integrity as a path to something more might look like.

Preaching Sample:
TAPPING INTO THE POWER OF INTEGRITY

SCRIPTURE TEXT: MATTHEW 8:5–10, 13

When [Jesus] entered Capernaum, a centurion approached him and appealed to him, saying, "Lord, my servant is lying at home paralyzed, suffering dreadfully." He said to him, "I will come and cure him." The centurion said in reply, "Lord, I am not worthy to have you enter under my roof; only say the word and my servant will be healed. For I too am a person subject to authority, with soldiers subject to me. And I say to one, 'Go,' and he goes; and to another, 'Come here,' and he comes; and to my slave, 'Do this,' and he does it." When Jesus heard this, he was amazed and said to those following him, "Amen I say to you, in no one in Israel have I found such faith. . . ." And Jesus said to the centurion, "You may go; as you have believed, let it be done for you." And at that very hour [his] servant was healed.

All talk, no action. I don't know about you, but in my household growing up, there were few worse statements that could be made about another person than that one. I can see my grandpa frowning at the television set when a campaign ad came on. I can see my dad reporting back from his fifth trip to the auto mechanic about the same rattling noise coming from under the hood. I can see my mom standing at the top of the basement stairway looking down on us kids who, having been sent down to clean up our toys over an hour ago, had still made no progress whatsoever. *All talk, no action.*

In contrast, there were few traits considered more praiseworthy in my household growing up than being a "man of your word." If my grandma described someone as a "man of his word" it meant you were okay to pay him in advance. My parents took giving their word so seriously that I cannot remember either of them ever saying something that they didn't follow through on. If they said they would bring brownies for my class party and the car wouldn't start (not unusual for a car that rattled incessantly), they'd bundle up all my younger siblings in the red wagon and walk a mile uphill in the snow to get me those brownies.

Now, lest you think the purpose of this preaching is to paint you a picture of Mayberry, I want to say that I suspect that Jesus and the centurion that we met in today's gospel were probably raised with similar values. Both were trained to take words seriously, because in both of their experiences, words meant action.

The centurion, if he didn't learn it at home, would certainly have learned it in the Roman military. A centurion was a Roman army leader who oversaw upward of a hundred soldiers and was personally responsible for their training and discipline. His men had to answer to him, just as he would have to answer to his superiors. If not, the punishment could be swift and harsh. His were words backed up by all the violent power and authority of the empire.

Jesus, I suspect, *did* learn it at home, growing up in a Jewish household that treasured the Word of God. From his earliest days, he would have heard his people's story of creation: "God said: Let there be light and there was light. . . . God said: Let us make human beings in our image" and there existed humankind in God's image (Gn 1:3, 26). He would have heard Isaiah: "My word shall not return to me empty, but shall do what pleases me, achieving the end for which I sent it" (Is 55:11).

He would know that all the way throughout scripture, word and action for God are one and the same thing, which is another way of saying—stay with me here—that God is utter integrity. What does *that* mean? It means there's no lying in God. There is no deceit in God. God is totally truthful, totally faithful. God's talk is all action. God is a "God of his word."

I'm not sure how old Jesus was when he discovered that God had shared that power with him—that he could tap into God's utter integrity and live out of that utter integrity. Integrity was such a different kind of power than what he would have seen in the wider Roman world. I wonder if he was surprised when he figured out that being totally honest, being consistently faithful to his words, made those words buzz with a divine authority. That his word alone could make things happen. I wonder if he kept this knowledge to himself for a while as he figured out how it all worked. But obviously he couldn't keep it completely hidden.

The centurion spotted it. He recognized that the power of Jesus' word was even more powerful than his own. His word as a centurion had the power to evoke action out of fear of repercussion, yes. But it had its limits. It couldn't multiply loaves. It couldn't raise the dead. And it couldn't heal his paralyzed servant. He may or may not have understood where the power of Jesus' word came from, but he knew that—even from afar—Jesus' word meant action.

I wonder how old you were when you figured out that people with integrity possess—or perhaps more accurately, participate in—a special kind of power. Maybe you've always known. Maybe, like me, you were blessed enough to be raised with great examples of it in your own home. Or maybe you had a teacher whose life buzzed with it. Or maybe you've only sensed the power of integrity from a distance in someone such as Pope Francis, Malala Yousafzai, or Mother Teresa. Maybe you would say that you are still waiting to meet someone of great integrity, someone whose words and actions are aligned in such a way that a special kind of energy radiates from them. You are still longing to see what integrity can do.

But even now, are you aware that *you* can tap into that power *yourself*? Whether you have any official status or not, whether you've got anyone reporting to you or not, you can nevertheless participate in the power of integrity. Even if no one else around you is doing it, *you* can be a person of your word. *You* can follow through on what you say. *You* can connect your words and your actions like a circuit and the electricity of God will start to buzz.

It'll probably befuddle others around you. They'll call the things that happen weird, extraordinary, occasionally even miraculous. And they will wonder how you seem to be able to just "make stuff happen." But you'll know. You'll know it really has nothing to do with you. You are but a conduit. When you live in such a way that your words and your actions are one, God will be able to do things in the world through you that an entire Roman army couldn't pull off.

But What If Others Aren't Truthful?

We can commit our own lips to only saying things that we believe to be true. We can work hard to make sure our words are aligned with our actions. At the same time, we recognize we live "among a people of unclean lips" (Is 6:5). If we were to espouse moral relativism, we might think, "Live and let live; it's none of our business." But lying is a "difference that makes a difference" in our capacity to function as a society, and people's lives are impacted by others' lies. Part of living truth involves working to make the world the kind of place where truthfulness is welcomed even when it is uncomfortable and where lying is discouraged rather than accepted. Beyond committing to greater truthfulness in our personal speech, we are asked as Catholics to work for greater truthfulness in our institutions, media, and governments. "An authentic faith . . ." says Pope Francis, "always involves a deep desire to change the world, to transmit values, to leave this earth somehow better than we found it" (*Evangelii Gaudium* 183). In *The Challenge of Forming Consciences for Faithful Citizenship*, the US Bishops confirm,

"In the Catholic Tradition, responsible citizenship is a virtue, and participation in political life is a moral obligation." As Catholics, we are expected to actively advocate for truthfulness and integrity in the public sphere.

In 2018, Pope Francis devoted his World Communications Day message to the topic of fake news, asking Christians at large, and journalists in particular, to help stop the spread of "false information based on non-existent or distorted data meant to deceive and manipulate the reader."[18] He identified in the current epidemic of fake news the same "snake-tactics" employed by "the 'crafty serpent' in the Book of Genesis, who, at the dawn of humanity, created the first fake news, which began the tragic history of human sin."[19] The pope encouraged efforts to educate people around characteristics of fake news and to pass laws curbing abuse.[20]

Living truth through public advocacy for truthfulness will feel uncomfortable for many in our congregations who would rather not get involved in controversial societal concerns. Indeed, many of us who preach share that discomfort. Hence, part of our task will be to make advocacy on behalf of truthfulness more imaginable and more manageable, with concrete small tasks that one can take on in daily life. Fortunately, scripture offers many models of ordinary people who found the courage to speak up about lies in their own times and can help us see the significance of such actions for the wider community. In the preaching that follows, I highlight the example of Daniel, whose story appears every year during Lent.

Preaching Sample:
DANIEL SPEAKS UP
MONDAY OF FIFTH WEEK OF LENT
SCRIPTURE TEXT:
DANIEL 13:41C–49

[The assembly] condemned [Susanna] to death. But Susanna cried aloud: "O Eternal God, you know what is hidden and are aware of all things before they come to be: you know that they have testified falsely against me. Here I am about to die, though I have done none of the things for which these men have condemned me."

The Lord heard her prayer. As she was being led to execution, God stirred up the holy spirit of a young boy named Daniel, and he cried aloud: "I am innocent of this woman's blood." All the people turned and asked him, "What are you saying?" He stood in their midst and said, "Are you such fools, you Israelites, to condemn a daughter of Israel without investigation and without clear evidence? Return to court, for they have testified falsely against her."

Each year the Church begins the fifth week of Lent with the lengthy retelling of Susanna's story, of which we have read just a small piece. Susanna was a married woman living in the Jewish diaspora community in Babylon following the exile. When she refuses the sexual advances of two elders in the community, they publicly accuse her of having an affair with an unknown suitor. They lie in court that they witnessed Susanna and her lover in the garden with each other. They claim the man was too strong and got away but that they caught Susanna in the act—an act punishable by death.

Susanna's execution is stayed only because a young man speaks up. A young judge named Daniel notes that someone is being accused "without investigation and without clear evidence." He refuses to be a part of it. He calls for a fair trial based on fact. When the elders are questioned separately, it becomes clear that their story is motivated by something other than truth, and Susanna survives to see another day.

The fact that the Church reads Susanna's story deep in the heart of Lent, on the edge of Holy Week, is not accidental. Clearly she is meant to remind us of another character who is falsely accused by the elders of his community, and that person would be Christ. Only two days ago in the gospel, we heard the elders of Jesus' day twisting his words to form accusations against him. One of those present, Nicodemus, made an effort similar to Daniel. "Does our law condemn a person before it first hears him and finds out what he is doing?" Nicodemus asked (Jn 7:51). But Nicodemus's voice is too faint, and it goes unheeded.

When the two stories are set side by side like this, we realize that the difference in outcome between Susanna and Christ is not due to the fact that one was innocent and the other was not but rather that one had a Daniel and the other did not. One had someone in her community willing to speak loudly and clearly on behalf of the importance of finding and telling the truth, and the other—as the story will continue to unfold in the week to come—had but fading support.

If you find your conscience pricked by reading Susanna's story, that's good. That's how it's supposed to be. By setting the story in this Lenten season, the Church is challenging us to look around and ask, "How outspoken am I in advocating for truthfulness in my community? Are there false accusations being made in my own time that I am content to let slide by thinking there is nothing I can do about them? Am I using my voice to call out for honesty or do I find myself fading into silence?" Just the fact that you are wondering such questions may be a sign that the Holy Spirit who arose in Daniel is trying to stir within you as well.

And it might not require anything big. It might require nothing more than a pen, a postcard, and a stamp—regularly writing your congressional representatives to let them know that you are a person who values truthfulness and you expect the same from them as your representative. It might mean gently nudging someone on your Facebook page, "Hey, I'm not sure you were aware of this, but I thought you'd want to know this story that you posted turns out not to be real. Here's a link so you can find out more." Maybe it means subscribing to something like Human Rights Watch or The Innocence Project to find out about persons who've been falsely accused of crimes for political purposes and writing letters on their behalf. Each of us can do *something* to stand up for the cause of truthfulness in our own community. For if we would not stand up for the Susannas of our own time, how can we say that we stand up for Christ?

A SUMMARY OF CHAPTER 3

Living in a post-truth society continues to raise challenging questions for those of us trying to pattern our lives after Jesus. Not only are we to ask ourselves, "What is truth?" and "How do I arrive at 'truths'?" but also "How do I speak and act truthfully? How do I align my words with my thoughts and my actions with my words?"

In order to enable our congregations to live truth in our current age, we will want to take every opportunity to:

- lift up the absolute necessity of truthfulness in speech if any society is to function and faith is to flourish;
- identify truthfulness as the gift of one's inner self to another that requires both a sense of justice and charity, in order to

navigate prudentially between saying too much and saying too little;
- be forthright about the sins of lying and hypocrisy as offenses against truthfulness;
- model integrity and authenticity in the way we present ourselves; and
- equip hearers to advocate for truthfulness and integrity in the wider society.

Truthfulness is never easy. But when we use words the way God uses words—truthfully loving and lovingly true—our words, like God's words, begin to be able to "do" things: We will find our words able to break through impasses. To heal. To set things free. Indeed, what we thought impossible becomes possible. It turns out "death and life" really have been all along "in the power of the tongue" (Prv 18:21).

For Reflection and Dialogue

- What kinds of guidelines help you know how much "truth" to tell from the pulpit, in the classroom, or in the boardroom? How do you know when you've said too much? How do you know if you've said too little?
- Because we preachers, teachers, and Church leaders speak so much publicly, we are naturally prone to charges of hypocrisy. How do you manage the tension of holding yourself accountable in your actions to the words you speak?
- What struggles do you see in your congregation related to truthfulness, lying, and hypocrisy? What have you tried to do previously to address these? How did it go? What would you do differently when you try it again?
- How would you assess the effectiveness of the preaching samples in this chapter in terms of the five markers of effectiveness named in the introduction to this book: having a single

message; using a conversational tone; specificity in language; valuing autonomy; and anticipating diversity of perspectives? What do you think might be done to heighten the samples' effectiveness?

- Is there anything that makes you nervous about trying to talk about truthfulness, lying, and hypocrisy in the current climate? What, if any, resistance do you find in yourself around drawing attention to these topics in preaching? What, if anything, would persuade you to try?

- Given the current political and ecclesial tensions related to these topics, what guidelines do you suggest for preachers concerning how to speak directly to situations of lying and hypocrisy? Would you have different advice for teachers or other Church leaders?

4.

Truth

AS A WAY OF BEING IN RELATIONSHIP

Imagine you were to ask me, "Is Mike true?" If I were a Greek philosopher and thinking about truth as it was introduced in the first chapter of this book, I might hear you questioning Mike's existence. Is he real or a figment of my imagination? But I am not a Greek philosopher; I am Mike's wife. I take for granted that Mike exists because I've been sleeping next to him for a quarter of a century. I see him at the breakfast table in the morning. We text or call each other on average five times a day. When I hear you ask, "Is Mike true?" I do not hear you wondering whether Mike exists; I hear you wondering whether Mike is faithful. Whether I can count on Mike. I think back to the morning that we stood in front of the church and promised to "be true" to each other "in good times and in bad, in sickness and in health, till death do us part." The word we use to ask about existence is the same, but obviously truth in the context of a long-lasting relationship means something different.

Our Jewish ancestors in the faith who scribed the Hebrew Scriptures were also not Greek philosophers. They were people who lived day in and day out a relationship with God that stretched back further than any of them could remember. As far as they were concerned, God was present at their breakfast table each morning. They did not write with the intention of trying to prove God's existence to those who did not believe in God; they wrote for family members, to record their memories of how God had been with them through thick and thin. They wrote to tell the story of their "marriage" with God—or to use the biblical term, their covenant. They wrote to reveal not *if* God was true (real) but *how* God was true (faithful).

The Hebrew word for truth—*emet*—appears in the Hebrew Scriptures 127 times. It comprises three Hebrew letters: *aleph*, the first letter of the Hebrew alphabet; *mem*, the letter in the middle of the Hebrew alphabet; and *tav*, the last letter of the Hebrew alphabet. All three of these letters have two "feet" that they stand upon, or two places where they touch the line upon which they are written. Scholars of the language emphasize that the very construction of the word says something about how our ancient ancestors in faith thought about truth: Truth encompasses everything from the beginning to the middle to the end. Truth is straightforward and comprehensible. In contrast, *sheker*—the Hebrew word for a lie—also comprises three letters, but all three come from the end of the alphabet and their order is jumbled. Each of the letters in *sheker* touch the line on which they are written only one time, as if they could easily be knocked over. But *emet* is well grounded, firm. It stands on two legs.

It is this last aspect of *emet* that makes it difficult to translate the word adequately in English. Yes, *emet* means much the same as what today's average person in the global West might associate with truth: grounded in reality, sound, honest. But *emet* has nuances beyond what we hear. *Emet* is sturdy, trustworthy, stable. *Emet* stands the test of time. If you lean on *emet*, it will hold you up. Hence, in English we find varied translations of the same lines in scripture. Depending on your Bible, Psalm 119:160 might say either "the sum of your word is truth" or "permanence is your word's chief trait." Jeremiah 7:28 can read that in the land of Judah "truth has perished" or "faithfulness has disappeared." To the Western ear these might sound quite different, but for our biblical ancestors, truth and faithfulness were synonymous. Truth is not only a way of thinking or speaking but also a way of being in a relationship.

This point—so often lost in societal debates about truth—has not been lost on Pope Francis. In his 2018 Chrism Mass homily, he talks about drawing close to people and being in relationship with them as "God's pedagogy." The pope states:

> We need to realize even more that closeness is . . . the key to truth. Can distances really be shortened where truth is concerned? Yes, they can. Because truth is not only the definition of situations and things from a certain distance, [discovered] by abstract and logical reasoning. It is more than that. Truth is also fidelity.[1]

As leaders who want to help our communities embrace truth as a way of life, the pope reminds us we cannot ignore this fourth way of understanding the term. Whatever spirituality of truth we propose would be fundamentally deficient without it. The good news is that this is the dimension of truth many of us already probably talk about the most without knowing that we are doing it. The challenge is merely to connect the preaching and teaching we are already doing to the larger framework of living truth. Many in our congregations will never have thought of truth in this way. Indeed, sometimes they will contrast truth with mercy. They will feel pulled between being faithful to a friend and telling them the truth. Our job is to help hearers understand that the contrasts they pose are two sides of the same coin. Living mercy will sometimes require offering the mercy of truth. And living truth will sometimes require hanging in there in relationships, even if we don't feel like it. In the preaching that follows, I offer a sample of what it might look like to highlight explicitly that elusive connection.

Preaching Sample:
PLIGHTING OUR TROUTHE

FIFTEENTH SUNDAY IN ORDINARY TIME YEAR C

SCRIPTURE TEXT: LUKE 10:30–35

A man fell victim to robbers as he went down from Jerusalem to Jericho. They stripped and beat him and went off leaving him half-dead. A priest happened to be going down that road, but when he saw him, he passed by on the opposite side. Likewise a Levite came to the place, and when he saw him, he passed by on the opposite side. But a Samaritan traveler who came upon him was moved with compassion at the sight. He approached the victim, poured oil and wine over his wounds and bandaged them. Then he lifted him up on his own animal, took him to an inn and cared for him. The next day he took out two silver coins and gave them to the innkeeper with the instruction, "Take care of him. If you spend more than what I have given you, I shall repay you on my way back."

Truth is a word we hear debated a lot in the news nowadays. We can have a hard time figuring out whether something is true. Whether a story we hear is true. Whether a statement is true. In the Church, whether a teaching is true. But when is the last time you asked what it means for a person to be true? The question rings a little odd in the ear, doesn't it? It forces my brain to flip a switch and recalculate what I mean by the word *truth*.

In medieval times, perhaps the question would not have sounded so odd. I was doing some research recently for a course on marriage that I'm teaching, and I was looking into the earliest form of wedding vows in the English language, which can be traced to the eleventh century.[2] The vows sounded remarkably similar to the ones we still use today—for richer, for poorer, in sickness and in health, etc.—until the last line, "I plight thee my trouthe."

"What on earth?" I thought. "What does it mean to plight my trouthe?" A little more reading helped me understand that we sometimes now translate the phrase as "I pledge you my truth," or perhaps even more commonly as "I promise to be faithful to you." "Ahhh," I thought. What a different way of thinking about the word *truth*. What I particularly loved about the original phrase that perhaps we've lost is the sense of "plight." There is a risk involved in promising fidelity to another. Truth isn't easy.

What I found fascinating was that it was not only married couples that would make such promises to one another. In the Middle Ages, friends, too, might decide to "trouthe-plight" one another. Innumerable poems and ballads from the eleventh up to the sixteenth centuries mention truth-pledging between "sworn brothers," occasionally also referred to as "wedded brothers." Friends sometimes took vows of fidelity on the steps of the church building—where early Christian marriages were conducted—before going inside to exchange the Sign of Peace and share Eucharist. Sworn friends were often buried side by side.[3]

Knowing these historical tidbits helped me understand much better why Pope Francis would raise the question of truth when he talked recently about the parable of the good Samaritan—the parable that we read as our gospel passage this morning.[4] For me, this most familiar of parables has never been about truth. It has been about mercy. It has been about being neighborly. It has been about charity. But not truth. Truth is about figuring out what is real and accurate. Truth is about taking a step back to get an objective picture of what is going on, so that we know how to act.

Yes, Francis says, truth is all of that, but truth is more than that. Truth is also about getting close to people. Like the Samaritan did. The priest and Levite assessed the situation from the opposite side of the road, perhaps not getting close enough to even tell that the man was still alive rather than dead. But what the Samaritan did was to draw near. He got close enough to the injured traveler that he could see what needed to be done. This wasn't knowledge that he arrived at from an objective analysis but a gut knowledge born of proximity. Truth is about the willingness to enter into a relationship, even if there might be a sense of plight involved.

Perhaps in all of our debate about truth nowadays, it is this older medieval—or even older, *biblical*—notion of truth where we should be focusing more of our attention: In these times of tension, do we remember how to *be* true to one another? Do we remember that there is a kind of knowing that we will glean not from textbooks or newspapers but only by drawing near to one another, by being in faithful relationships with one another, by taking risks for one another?

There is nothing in the good Samaritan parable to indicate that the Samaritan made a permanent vow to the injured traveler, but in some ways we could say that he exemplifies what it means to "trouthe-plight" another—to be faithful to another in time of deep, deep need. And perhaps he can be a model for us this week as we figure out what it means to do truth in our daily lives, amid our families and friends, in our own neighborhoods and in our travels. Rather than run away, take a risk. Draw near and trust you will know what to do.

IS TRUTH JUST ANOTHER WORD FOR LOYALTY?

Once we begin to foster a connection between truth and particular relationships, many in our congregations may immediately associate the truth we are talking about with loyalty. *Loyalty* is an interesting term. Currently in the English language it is defined as having an allegiance to a person, a group, or a cause. Like faithfulness, it implies rooting for another, sticking with another even if one doesn't necessarily benefit from doing so. In everyday usage, though, it often implies a willingness to take the other's side, to publicly defend the other regardless of the rightness or wrongness of their actions. There is no exact equivalent for loyalty in either Hebrew or Greek, so the term appears rarely in the Bible, though some translations do use it to capture the essence of the word *hesed* (also translated "loving-kindness") or *pistos* (also translated "faithful"). Although there is a Latin equivalent of the term—*fidelitas*—the word does not appear in Thomas Aquinas's *Summa Theologiae*. He does not name loyalty as a virtue. The closest he comes to describing what we might call loyalty is in his writing on what he labels *piety*.

What the wider Judeo-Christian tradition seems to recognize is that allegiance is a good thing, but only so far as the person or cause that I pledge myself to is good. There is no virtue in being

loyal to a criminal gang. Furthermore, there is no virtue in publicly
standing up and defending the actions of a friend or family member who has done something you would judge as wrong. Rather
than talking about loyalty, the tradition tends to describe being true
in terms of *devotion, fidelity, faithfulness,* or *steadfastness.* All of these
words imply an allegiance, but not necessarily an uncritical one.
The emphasis is not on standing by the other person regardless
but on being the kind of person that one can lean on regardless.
Not being unquestionably trusting but being utterly trustworthy.

For one looking to nurture a spirituality of truth, the whole of
the Hebrew Scriptures emerges as the story of a God who is true
to the people of Israel. However, the scriptures do not describe a
God who stands by and supports the people as they do whatever
they please. God loves the people too much not to care where their
actions lead. Rather, God gets angry and frustrated. God cajoles
and pleads. God often laments. God constantly calls them to be
their better selves. God forgives and lets bygones be bygones. The
only constant is that God remains with the people and does not
abandon them. God is faithful to relationship with them, even
when they are not faithful in return.

But in their better moments, they *are* faithful—and in glorious
ways. In one of the most moving passages in the Hebrew Scriptures, the Babylonian king Nebuchadnezzar, commands three
Jewish employees of his government—Shadrach, Meshach, and
Abednego—to bow down before a statue of himself or be thrown
into a fiery pit. "Who is the God who can deliver you [then]?"
Nebuchadnezzar asks (Dn 3:15). In reply, the three note that their
relationship with God is not dependent on God doing their bid-
ding: "If our God, whom we serve, can save us from the white-hot
furnace and from your hands, O king, may he save us! *But even if
he will not,* you should know, O king, that we will not serve your
god or worship the golden statue which you set up" (Dn 3:17–18,
emphasis added). Regardless of whether God rescues them or not,
they have decided to be faithful to God. Many of the passages we

are given to preach upon will flesh out the deep and abiding fidelity the people of Israel have shown their God, a fidelity that surely shaped Jesus' own understanding of being true and is meant to shape ours as well.

In the preaching sample that follows, I explore one of Jesus' key images of what it means to be steadfast in a relationship, a much richer concept than simply being loyal.

Preaching Sample:
ON REMAINING
FIFTH SUNDAY OF EASTER
YEAR B

SCRIPTURE TEXT:
JOHN 15:1–8

[Jesus said to his disciples:] "I am the true vine, and my Father is the vine grower. He takes away every branch in me that does not bear fruit, and everyone that does he prunes so that it bears more fruit. You are already pruned because of the word that I spoke to you. Remain in me, as I remain in you. Just as a branch cannot bear fruit on its own unless it remains on the vine, so neither can you unless you remain in me. I am the vine, you are the branches. Whoever remains in me and I in him will bear much fruit, because without me you can do nothing. Anyone who does not remain in me will be thrown out like a branch and wither; people will gather them and throw them into a fire and they will be burned. If you remain in me and my words remain in you, ask for whatever you want and it will be done for you. By this is my Father glorified, that you bear much fruit and become my disciples."

This past Saturday we buried my uncle, who I know that many of you have heard me pray for week after week over the course of the past couple months. Even though he was married to my aunt for almost forty years and I was in their wedding as flower girl at the tender age of five, I wouldn't say I knew him particularly well. But what I do know is the way my aunt and my cousins hung with him even as he diminished before our eyes, first losing the right side of his jaw and then part of his lung, his hair, his eyebrows, his strength, his vigor, his vitality, and finally his hope for any sort of recovery. When there was really nothing more that could be done, it frustrated some of us—can't we bring more food, more prayers, more fuzzy blankets? No, the freezer, linen closet, and even spiritual bouquet were stocked.

When I brought his daughter from the airport last week, she walked into the bedroom and said, "Is there anything you need, Dad?" and he simply pointed to the space next to him in the bed. She lay down at his side and put her head on his shoulder. "Closer," he said. She scooched more. "Closer," he said again. "I can't," she stated, "or I'd be right on top of you, and I don't want to hurt you." "I'd be okay with that," he said as a tear rolled down his cheek. And a tear rolled down hers.

I've thought about this moment a lot in the past week. In the end, we don't want blankets, food, or even—dare I say—prayers. We want those we love close to us—so close that they become one with us. We can't get them close enough. The deepest human desire is not for stuff—even the basic stuff we need to stay alive and comfortable. The deepest human desire is for communion. To love and to be loved; to dwell in love.

Is it really any surprise that Jesus would express this desire himself on the night before he died? There were no more trips to take to the Temple. No more fishing expeditions on the Sea of Galilee to be had. No more "calling" and "following" and "inviting 'Come!'" His last request . . . his deepest desire was that we simply remain with him, in him.

It seems like such a simple thing: just remain. Really? That's all you want me to do, just be with you? Rest with you? Rest in you? Not serve you? Not make great sacrifices for you? Not move mountains for you? Really, just "remain" in you?

Simple indeed. That is, until we try it. At which point we discover that remaining is among the most difficult activities that we can ever undertake. Sometimes it can be an immensely pleasurable activity, just to be in the presence of someone you love and spend time with them. But it also requires the capacity to still be there, even when you are bored of looking into their eyes and bored of hearing them tell the same story for the umpteenth time when you would rather be watching TV or attacking your massive to-do list.

And sometimes it requires staying in the same room when you are so angry with them you could spit. It means continuing to talk and to share your feelings, even when those feelings are ugly and tangled and it'd be easier to create a wall of silence twelve feet thick. And sometimes—as I saw last week—remaining means you will see people you love in tremendous pain and that is such an uncomfortable place to be. Or it means *being seen* in all one's weakness, vulnerability, and need, which for some of us is probably the hardest of all.

We often talk as if "going" requires the greatest strength. We admire those who run marathons and travel to faraway exotic places, sacrificing life and limb to conquer the frontiers of human capacity. But, truthfully, the greater strength is not in going; it is in remaining. And unless we nurture the capacity for remaining in ourselves, we will never taste the communion that every fiber of our being longs for. We will conquer the highest mountains and the greatest distances, but we will still come up short. We might do incredible activities. We might be outrageously busy. But—to paraphrase the great Dominican Dalmazio Mongillo—these good works will be like ornaments hung on a Christmas tree rather than like fruit blossoming on the vine, as Jesus describes. In the end, communion isn't just what we want most but rather what we were actually created *for*.

Sometimes you know a sermon is coming to the end when the preacher arrives at the action step—the "here is what the Bible wants you to do" step. There will be none of that this week. There is nothing Jesus wants you to do this week at all. All Jesus asks is that you remain.

Shouldn't I Also Worry about Being True to Myself?

The phrase "To thine own self be true" certainly sounds like the sort of thing we might find in the Bible, and the sort of thing that then might be a crucial component of this fourth dimension of truth that we are talking about. Many in our communities will assume this to be the case. Nowadays the phrase is often used to mean "Make sure that you are being honest with yourself," "Do the right thing; not what everyone else around you is doing," or "You are a unique person; don't try to be someone else." All sentiments aligned with Christian thought. The phrase, however, comes not from the Bible but Shakespeare, in the tragedy *Hamlet*.[5] It first appears in the mouth of the character Polonius, who uses it to advise his son, "Watch out for your own interests first." Current use of the phrase often carries those undertones as well: "Don't let other people keep you down; do what's best for you." "Listen to your body and go with your gut." "Don't stay in relationships that aren't working for you." These are all sentiments that rub up in some ways against Christian teaching.

From a biblical point of view, each of us is made in the image and likeness of God, but each of us has also been born into a fallen world and continues to participate in deeply embedded patterns of sin. In this biblical sense, our true self is not something fixed that we have to discover and be faithful to. Our true self is something that we are always moving toward, by the grace of Baptism—continually turning away from a life marked by sin toward a life that looks like Christ's. The apostle Paul is especially forceful on this point: "So whoever is in Christ is a new creation: the old things have passed away; behold, new things have come" (2 Cor 5:17).

In his letters, Paul admonishes hearers not to trust their "flesh"[6] because it will take them backward rather than forward on this Christian journey. What Paul means by "flesh" is not an exact parallel for what many now would call "gut," but it is also not entirely different. I suspect that most of us who currently work in the field of spirituality and discernment would say that feelings are very important. Because we are made in the image and likeness of God, the gut is a valuable source of information. It's worth listening to your body and being attentive to what it is trying to tell you. But until our guts are entirely conformed to Christ, it should not be the determining factor for our choices in life, and I don't think that many of us could currently say our guts have achieved that level of development. Feelings can give us a clue—"Hey, something important is happening here"—but they shouldn't dictate our actions.

Since Christianity views the self as something always in the process of conversion, being *true to self* is not language that is used historically in the Catholic tradition. In places where contemporary culture might appeal to the notion of being true to self, the tradition is more likely to appeal to *conscience, the dignity of the human person,* or *the image and likeness of God,* while adding caution or nuance around anything that makes it sound as if we should put ourselves before others or make decisions on our gut sense, absent some larger moral code. If we decide to use the term (since it is so very common in the culture), we'll want to do so with caution. It seems to me that we don't want to speak against being true to self. Self-awareness and integrity are virtues we espouse. We can't love our neighbor if we haven't learned how to love and value ourselves. At the same time, we don't want to offer a blanket endorsement of being true to self. Being self-centered and impulse-driven are vices. Like relativism, the way the phrase is used in contemporary culture is too ambiguous in meaning to be advocated or condemned without further clarification: Are we talking here about fidelity to the old Adam or the new?

One of the most challenging contemporary uses of the phrase has to do with how we use it when trying to decide whether to stay in a tough relationship. The temptation is to pit being true to another person against being true to oneself. Figuring out what to do in tough relationships is, well . . . tough. The judgments we make about relationships can be some of the toughest judgments we have to make in our lives. But from a Christian point of view, being true to self is too amorphous a concept to rely on as a guide in such situations.

But What Does Truth Look Like When We Disagree . . . and Maybe Don't Even Like Each Other Anymore?

Being true has little to do with agreeing or feeling affection. The pages of scripture and the lives of the saints are filled with stories of people who figured out how to remain in relationship with God, with others, and with causes and organizations even when they didn't always see eye to eye and wearied of the relationship itself. As initially highlighted in chapter 1, the first impulse of the tradition seems to be "Try to hang in there." This impulse should guide not only our ongoing search for facts and our struggle to form good judgments but also our relationships with people. The practices for talking across differences of opinion discussed in chapter 2 are intended to help us refine our thinking and broaden our understanding. As an added bonus, they also give us a way of faithfully remaining in relationships when it would be easier to opt out. They help us hang in there with both the conversation and the relationship itself.

But what about when it no longer makes sense to continue the conversation? What can we do when we've listened and understand where the other is coming from but we still don't agree? Being true does not require continuing to beat our head against a brick wall. There are ways of hanging in the relationship even if not in the conversation. We can still:

- will the best for the other, even when the other appears headed in the wrong direction
- remain in the present moment and not hold on to unresolved disagreements from the past in such a way that they continue to poison the present relationship
- look for common ground by identifying topics we *can* agree on and focusing our energy on those
- pray for one another
- engage in activities of daily life with each other, especially joint service and shared hobbies
- seek opportunities to do an act of kindness for the other
- avoid ultimatums except as a last resort

In our preaching, we can lift up stories of people hanging in the best that they are able. Many of the saints that we celebrate during the liturgical year provide great models of remaining faithful to marriages, friendships, religious communities, or the Church itself, without losing their integrity in the process. These are important stories for our congregations to hear, as they try to figure out creative ways of being true to their consciences and to particular relationships simultaneously.

At the same time, we have to acknowledge—albeit with sadness—that not all relationships on this side of eternity are sustainable. God has the capacity to be faithful to people in ways that we as humans do not. Sometimes patterns of abuse, addiction, and even profound, sustained differences of perception make it untenable to stay actively engaged in even a committed relationship. Every community, cause, and person must have boundaries on what stances and behaviors they are able to tolerate and, in the end, what they cannot.

Vows of fidelity are taken particularly seriously in the Christian tradition. They are promises intended to create relationships so solid that the community can build upon them and trust they will not crumble.[7] Vows are for life. But even that statement needs to be understood in two ways. Vows are meant to be permanent, but they are also intended in the plan of God to be *life-giving* for the persons who take them and for the community. If they lead to the disintegration of the person and the harm of the community, then they have stopped serving the purpose for which they are created.[8] We can continue to pray for each other, try to let go of past hurts, and wish each other the best—remaining true in the most fundamental of ways. But sometimes we will need to step back from an active relationship until circumstances change, not because we are being "true to self" out of selfishness but rather we are trying to be "true to self" out of a sense of integrity. Ultimately this is a decision that will need to be made between the person and God.

No matter how well we know our hearers, we never know all the circumstances of their lives. Aware of that fact, I think we want to resist the temptation to tell people to stay or go in relationships. From the pulpit, we can lift up the value of fidelity, as well as the importance of vows, and then we want to honor the autonomy of hearers to figure out what this means in their own particular situations. Perhaps the best we can do is offer models of what staying and what going look like. Even if they are imperfect models, they can serve as companions on our hearers' journeys.

The preaching sample that follows was originally offered in a community of vowed religious men—many still in formation—in the wake of another revelation of clergy sexual abuse in the media. In it, I try to acknowledge the significance of the commitments they have made; the depth of disappointment and anger they may feel in the Church they've committed themselves to; and the questions they may be wondering about whether to stay or go, realizing there is no single answer to this question. (While I do think that preaching as a norm should be rooted in a scripture text, on occasion I will use the writing of a saint as the base text in a Liturgy of the Hours service. The following is an example of such a choice.)

Preaching Sample:
CARRYING THE SHIP
FEAST OF CATHERINE OF SIENA

FROM THE LAST LETTER OF CATHERINE, TO RAYMOND OF CAPUA

The fire increased more and more in me and I had only one thought: what I could do to offer up myself to God for Holy Church and to deliver those whom God had given into my hands from ignorance and negligence. Then the devils shouted death upon me and would hinder and repress my desire which filled them with terror. And they struck hard at me, but my desire grew freer and stronger, and I cried:

"O, eternal God, accept my life as a sacrifice for the mystical body of Holy Church. I can give nothing but what Thou hast given me Thyself. Take the heart then. Take the heart and press out the blood of it over the face of the Bride." Then God looked in mercy upon me and He tore out the heart and pressed it out over Holy Church. And He seized it with such force that if He had not at once girded me about with His strength—for he would not that the vessel of my body should be broken—I should have passed hence. . . . But hell has no power against the strength of humility and the light of holy faith; I collected my thoughts the more and labored as though with glowing irons; before the face of God, I heard words so sweet and promises that filled me with joy. And because it was all so hidden my tongue is no longer able to speak of it. . . . We shall conquer the devil, not by the suffering itself borne in our bodies, but by virtue of that fire which is divine and exceedingly ardent and inestimable love. *Deo gratias*, Amen. *Gesu dolce, Gesu amore.*

As a child, I was deeply enchanted with the orange St. Joseph edition of *Catholic Saints for Boys and Girls*. There were several St. Catherines in this book, and it was difficult to keep them all straight. The easiest one to distinguish was Catherine Labouré. She wore a most unusual hang-glider-like contraption on her head and looked as though she might be whipped away upon the next gust of wind. Second in line, however, was Catherine of Siena. She was fairly easy to spot because she was always carrying a large wooden boat on her shoulder. I wondered what that was all about. Growing up, I met many people who walked around with a chip on their shoulder, but never anyone with a ship on their shoulder!

Until recently I had assumed that the ship was an iconographer's invention—a symbol of the role that Catherine had played in steering the Church through the rocky waters of the Avignon papacy. Only in rereading the story of Catherine's life this past week did I realize that the image of Catherine bearing the boat was not an artist's creation but one deeply rooted in Catherine's own imagination—based on an event that took place shortly before her death, shortly before the letter we read tonight was written.

The early months of 1380 found Catherine in Rome, praying for the new pope Urban, hopeful that reform was imminent, worried that it was not. These months found Catherine daily in the original St. Peter's Basilica, before the tomb of the first apostle. Catherine fixated upon Giotto's mosaic of the apostles' humble fishing vessel—an image of *la Navicella*.

One Sunday during Vespers, her disciple Tommaso Caffarini testifies, "While the winter evening began to creep in over the city," Catherine watched the bark leave the mosaic and come to rest squarely on her shoulders. Her companions saw nothing, but witnessed the fragile, thin Catherine collapse to the ground as if crushed by its weight. She was paralyzed and had to be carried home. She never recovered, and three months later, she died.

There was a time when flying boats would have rubbed me the wrong way. There was a time when much of Catherine of Siena's story would have rubbed me the wrong way. And still, if Catherine were one of my ministry students, it is unlikely she would pass. We'd have to have some conversations about the virtues of living a healthy, balanced life; about dealing with guilt and grief; about psychosomatic manifestations. Catherine's spirituality emerged out of a cultural and historical context very different from our own, and our ideas about what marks holiness have continued to shift over time.

And yet, for all our language about balance, health, and self-care, chances are that when we reflect on the conclusion of Catherine's life and writings on her feast day *this* year, we are not rubbed wrongly but rather sympathetically. We know a little more this year about the weight of *la Navicella*. We understand a little better this year what it means to carry that weight on one's shoulders. We identify a little more this year with what it is like to be crushed by free-falling mosaics.

For some in society, the weight of *la Navicella* is something that they see in the newspaper on the shoulders of a stooped pope. For most in this room, though—among the ministerial class of the Church—it is something not only witnessed from afar but also carried in the innermost recesses of the heart. A deep sadness. A gravest of worries. A blackest of fears. A crushing, almost paralyzing weight.

And we know it'd be smarter to run. That no good can come from propping up with our own bodies a ship that seems so determined to sink. That soon ministerial leadership will be ranked up there with smoking and race car driving as a life insurance risk. But against all our better judgment, we don't. We can't.

Instead we find ourselves praying crazy things in the middle of the night, such as "Use me, Lord. I offer my whole self on behalf of this Church. And if I had a thousand lives, every one of them would be given to this people. And if I had a thousand magic wishes, every one of them would be for their healing. Let me be of service however I can, even if it means I suffer. Take this heart, Lord, and pour it out over your Church."

As if we had the heart of Christ living inside us or something. And maybe we do.

Maybe we realize that perhaps Catherine was not so different after all. Or perhaps we are crazier than we thought.

This is the craziness of love. It's the craziness that allows marriages to last fifty-plus years. The craziness that allows parents to last through the teenage years. The craziness that allows religious to celebrate diamond jubilee years. The craziness that allows the Church to survive more than two thousand years. It's the craziness that perpetuates creation, that breathes life into the dead, that hopes for a new day every day. This is the crazy, salvific love of God.

And it is a mystery to us. It is a mystery how that which we love so much might end up crushing us. And how that which crushes us gives us life. And it's hard to know when God's desire that we have abundant life means we must go. And when God's desire that all have abundant life means we must stay.

Perhaps Catherine is not the best of models in this decision. After all, she died emaciated and tormented at the age of thirty-three. This is not anything that I would wish for any of us. But Catherine is perhaps the best of companions on this journey along the tightrope of ecclesial life—someone who knows exactly our struggles to be faithful, truthful, and loving in this community, even if it kills us. Someone who can empathize tenderly with the weight we carry, as we stand in reverence of the weight she carried.

Of the many saintly Catherines we might befriend in our tradition—from Alexandria to Bologna to Sweden—this frail yet fiery woman from Siena is one to whom we should wish to draw near right now. For she will teach us about the excruciating paradoxes of love—"divine and exceedingly ardent, and inestimable love."

Deo gratias, Amen. *Gesu dolce, Gesu amore.*

But How Can We Be True to Everyone?

Many in our communities are people of tremendous fidelity. They *want* to be true in good times and bad. The internal struggle they face with regard to this fourth dimension of truth isn't the fruit of an unwillingness to be true to others but a sense of overwhelm: "How can we be true to everyone?" The answer: We can't. God can because God exists without limits in terms of time and resources. But we are human.

For the past thirty years, University of Oxford professor Robin Dunbar has been studying human relationships, looking in particular at the number of relationships humans tend to engage in at any one time. Using research from the field of biology that correlates the size of a primate's brain with the size of that primate's social network, Dunbar hypothesized that, based on the size of the human brain, the average human would have a social network of around 150 people.[9] When he looked at historical data, he discovered his hypothesis strangely accurate: The average hunter-gatherer community tended to be around 150 people. The average Roman military company was around 150 people. The average village recorded in the *Domesday Book* of AD 1086 was around 150 people. To this day, the Christmas card list for a British couple averages 150 people.

Dunbar observes that at any point in time we will have a larger circle of acquaintances with whom we keep loose contact—up to 500 people. And persons are able to hold up to 1,500 faces with names in their brains—news personalities, distant relatives, old classmates, and the like. But they are only able to maintain ongoing relationships with about 150. Within that 150, Dunbar notes persons usually have around fifteen close relationships, and only around five intimates in the innermost circle. Who is in each of these concentric circles is fluid and changes over time, but the size of the circles tends to remain the same because it is all our brains can juggle.

Many have asked whether Dunbar's research is still valid given the rise of social media. With WhatsApp and Instagram, we are able to keep up with far more people than we ever did before. Dunbar acknowledges that some relational trends seem to be shifting.

Historically, humans spent 60 percent of their time with their closest circles of family and friends and 40 percent in wider circles of acquaintances. Those percentages may now be reversing, but Dunbar suspects limitations remain. "The amount of social capital you have is pretty fixed," he says. "[Relationships] involve time investment. If you garner connections with more people, you end up distributing your fixed amount of social capital more thinly so the average capital per person is lower."[10]

Biologically we are not wired to be able to maintain personal relationships with an infinite number of people. We can be conscious of the fact that we all live on the same planet, and conscientious about the way that our actions affect others. Through charitable giving we can be generous with persons we have never met. We can even be *friendly* to everyone that we do meet. But we can't *be friends* with everyone. As creatures bound in earthly time, we will need to make some choices: "How do I decide who I am supposed to be true to? How do I prioritize how devoted to be in the various relationships in my life?"

Obviously we are not the first generation to feel the constraints life puts on our desire to be in relationship. In the fifth century CE, Augustine of Hippo acknowledged that "all men are to be loved equally. But since you cannot do good to all, you are to pay special regard to those who, by the accidents of time, or place, or circumstance, are brought into closer connection with you."[11] Thomas Aquinas similarly notes we are called to be equally *benevolent* toward all—in essence, we are called to want the best for all. Indeed, we can pray for all.[12] But our *beneficence*—our *doing* good for others—realistically cannot be equal toward all, though he says we should "be prepared . . . to do good to anyone if we have time to spare."[13] (Interesting that even in the Middle Ages Aquinas understood the time crunch!) Like Augustine, Aquinas notes that, just as in nature "fire heats most what is next to it,"[14] we owe the greatest devotion to those closest to us and should radiate outward from there. In Aquinas's understanding, our first "truth" must be to God, then to our parents (extending to all kinfolk), and then to our fellow countrymen (eventually extending to all friends of our country).[15]

It seems important to note that both Augustine and Aquinas lived in a time when most people were bound by not only time but also geography. When they speak of being most devoted to those closest to you, they were likely thinking quite literally of the people with whom one would have the most physical contact. At that time, persons who were poor, suffering, ill, or disabled were in the mix of those encountered daily. Now, with the development of institutions such as hospitals and nursing homes, as well as the emergence of urban planning, we may not see these people in our daily mix. Jesus said that the poor would "always be with us," but now often it is at a distance of at least several miles.

Furthermore, in the time of Augustine and Aquinas, when someone moved away, there was no way of remaining in sustained contact with that person, opening up space for new relationships to form. Now, because of apps such as Facetime and Facebook, those at a distance do not feel so far away. It is possible to communicate daily, even hourly, with people we rarely see in person while paying little attention to those with whom we share physical proximity.

On one hand, the benefits of technology for maintaining relationships at a distance are amazing. On the other hand, we could ask, what happens when we disconnect emotional closeness from physical closeness? Certainly we can keep some treasured relationships going that we might otherwise have lost. But who are we then *not* relating to? Who is *not* making it into our 150?

Perhaps what we can take from Augustine and Aquinas is the acknowledgment that it is natural and understandable to prioritize some relationships over others. We cannot be equally true to all. *Phew!* At the same time, in an era when there are fewer of Augustine's "accidents of time, place, and circumstance" and we have more control over who we connect with every day, are we making space for those who are now on the margins of society?

Like everyone else, those who are poor, suffering, ill, or disabled desire not just friendliness but friendship. Everybody wants to be part of *somebody's* 150. The preaching sample that follows attempts to address this tension, inviting hearers to consider who they allow into their circle of friendship and who might be without a circle. Like Bartimaeus, the Syrophoenician woman, and the Roman centurion from earlier chapters, Jesus tells the hemorrhaging woman that it is her faith that has saved her. Once again, in this episode, it is the woman's faith that Jesus' circle of concern could widen to include her.

Preaching Sample:
WHO WILL YOU ALLOW TO TOUCH YOU?

THIRTEENTH SUNDAY IN ORDINARY TIME YEAR B

SCRIPTURE TEXT: MARK 5:25–34

There was a woman afflicted with hemorrhages for twelve years. She had suffered greatly at the hands of many doctors and had spent all that she had. Yet she was not helped but only grew worse. She had heard about Jesus and came up behind him in the crowd and touched his cloak. She said, "If I but touch his clothes, I shall be cured." Immediately her flow of blood dried up. She felt in her body that she was healed of her affliction. Jesus, aware at once that power had gone out from him, turned around in the crowd and asked, "Who has touched my clothes?" But his disciples said to him, "You see

> how the crowd is pressing upon you, and yet you ask, 'Who touched me?'" And he looked around to see who had done it. The woman, realizing what had happened to her, approached in fear and trembling. She fell down before Jesus and told him the whole truth. He said to her, "Daughter, your faith has saved you. Go in peace and be cured of your affliction."

The gospel of the day paints a familiar scene: a crowd pressed in around Jesus, jostling him from every side. In the midst of the chaos, however, we hear that Jesus suddenly becomes aware of the fact that a woman has touched him—a woman with a significant need that had affected her (as illnesses so often do) both physically and financially, exhausting her resources.

And Jesus asks, "Who touched me?"

Jesus' friends find it a ridiculous question. Hundreds of people are likely to have rubbed up against him. How are they supposed to know? But Jesus is insistent, his eyes searching through the crowd to identify the one, to acknowledge the one.

There is a difference between being jostled and being touched. Jesus knew it when he experienced it, and I suspect we do too. The difference, however, is mysterious. It generally has not so much to do with the sort of physical contact, because both could look pretty similar to the outsider observing the interaction. Rather, it has to do with the receptiveness of the one who is confronted by someone in need. Sometimes people on the street jostle us. And once in a while, they touch us. The difference is likely less within them and more within us.

I was reading recently about the life of Jean Vanier, the founder of the L'Arche movement that has created homes around the world for adults with and without intellectual disabilities to live in community with one another. Maybe you've heard of Vanier before or visited one of these L'Arche communities. What I didn't know before reading was that this now sizable international movement began when Vanier, a former Navy officer and budding academic, was visiting a psychiatric hospital south of Paris. It was not a pleasant place. Lots and lots of people were housed there, hidden from the rest of society. Surely there were many distressed residents jostling for Vanier's attention as he walked through the space. But for some reason, there were two men that day that he later couldn't get out of his mind. Vanier realized the men were being taken care of physically but that "essentially, they wanted a friend. They were not very interested in my knowledge or my ability to do things, but rather they needed my heart and my being."[16] He ended up buying a home where the three of them could live together.

Who touched Jean Vanier? Raphaël Simi and Philippe Seux—two men with disabilities now considered the cofounders of the L'Arche movement. One hundred and fifty L'Arche homes later, Vanier writes, "The cry for help and the trust that springs up from the heart of a fragile person give him or her a secret power that can open many a closed heart. The weakest can activate forces of loving generosity that are hidden in the hearts of the strong."[17] If, that is, we allow ourselves to be touched.

This week, if your mailbox is anything like mine, you will receive innumerable envelopes asking for donations. On top of that, you will likely receive any number of unsolicited phone calls and encounter any number of persons face to face asking for help. Many of these encounters will undoubtedly feel like jostling, hassling. There really is no way to help out everyone who asks and no way to get to know everyone who is in need. We each have to figure out how to prioritize our limited resources of money, time, and energy. We can't get involved in every good cause or stop to form a relationship with everyone we meet. But it is also worth asking, "Have I allowed *anyone* in need to touch me recently?" And I'm not saying, "Have I handed anyone a dollar on the street?" but rather, "Have I allowed someone to actually touch me? Have I allowed anyone's story to slow me down long enough to listen deeply? Is there anyone's plight that I've permitted to stop me in my tracks lately?"

Perhaps we could pause for a moment right now and make Jesus' question our own: "Who touched me?" And perhaps this is a question that we could commit to continue asking each night this coming week, perhaps this coming month. Before going to bed, just pause and ask, "Who touched me today?" If we realize there is no one, we could ask, "Who could I have allowed to touch me today?" In becoming aware of how we answer that question each day, I suspect patterns might begin to emerge. And, like Vanier, we will get clues as to where God might be leading us next in life. Not to everyone but at least to someone.

A SUMMARY OF CHAPTER 4

Living in a post-truth society continues to raise challenging questions for those of us trying to pattern our lives after Jesus—not only "What is truth?" and "How do I arrive at 'truths'?" and "How do I speak and act truthfully?" but also, in the end, "What does it mean to be true?" In essence, "What does it mean to be faithful in a relationship and why should I care?" Without addressing this final dimension of living truth, whatever spirituality of truth we attempt to cultivate in our preaching, teaching, and leading will be incomplete.

Drawing on the wisdom of our Jewish ancestors in the faith concerning truth as *emet,* in the acts of preaching, teaching, and leading within the Church we want to

- foster a connection in the minds of hearers between being faithful in relationships and living truth;
- highlight that being true in a relationship is not the same as uncritical loyalty, agreement, or even affection toward the other person;
- encourage the kinds of skills and capacities needed to remain in relationships, which includes communication skills but also other ways of remaining in relationships when we've reached impasses in conversations; and
- acknowledge that we can't be true equally to everyone and aren't expected to be, while encouraging hearers to stretch their circles of friendship to include those who might not otherwise enjoy friendship.

As with the discernment of reality, the formation of judgments, or figuring out how much to say to whom, living truth in relationships does not come with a foolproof how-to guide, only a well-worn map by which we can trace the paths our ancestors in faith took as they tried to faithfully live their own relationships. We discover in the words of Dostoevsky, "Love in action is a harsh and dreadful thing compared with love in dreams. Love in dreams is greedy for immediate action, rapidly performed and in the sight of all. Men will even give their lives if only the ordeal does not last long but is soon over. . . . But love is labor and fortitude."[18] We remain grateful for our ancestors' witness to this deep truth.

For Reflection and Dialogue

- What are the relationships to which you have been most true in your own life? What guidelines help you know how much "truth" you owe to a particular relationship? How do you discern whether to hang in a relationship or whether to pull away?
- How often does the theme of fidelity in relationships already appear in your preaching, teaching, or leading? In what ways

have you made the connection between fidelity and truth before? How could you imagine making this connection stronger?

- What struggles do you see in your community in terms of being true in their relationships? What have you tried to do previously to address these concerns? How did it work? How might you do things differently if you had the chance to do it over?
- How would you assess the effectiveness of the preaching samples in this chapter in terms of the five markers of effectiveness named in the introduction to this book: having a single message; using a conversational tone; specificity in language; valuing autonomy; and anticipating diversity of perspectives? What do you think might heighten the samples' effectiveness?
- What, if anything, makes you nervous about trying to talk about being true in the current climate? Do you find any resistance in yourself around drawing attention to these topics in preaching? Can you name that resistance? What would persuade you to overcome it and give talking about being true a try?

5.

Truth,

NEXT STEPS

In this book we've explored four distinct, albeit intertwined, ways the Catholic tradition thinks about truth, each playing a role in nurturing what we might call a spirituality of truth or living truth. In organizing the material this way, I admit that I have made a complicated subject perhaps simpler than it is. Where the line is drawn between facts and judgments, for example, is not always very clear. Even when I state what appears to be a simple fact, such as "Columbus discovered America in 1492," a careful thinker might rightly ask, "Why do you say 'Columbus'? Were there not others on the boat? When you say 'discovered' do you mean that there weren't people already there? 'America' according to whom? Did not the indigenous peoples already have a name for the land on which they lived? 'In 1492'—according to which calendar?" The language I choose when trying to relay facts always embeds within it some degree of judgment such that while reality might be objective my description of it is not.

Furthermore, it would be good and right to ask whether there are ways for stories to be "true to reality" even if they are not factually true. Fictional literature often resonates as true to life even as we know the events therein didn't happen. In what way is Aesop's fable of the tortoise and the hare true? Or, of particular concern to us who preach and teach, the ancient stories of creation and the flood found in the Bible? By what rubric do we determine the truthfulness of a poem, metaphor, or myth?

There is so much more that could be explored regarding the topic of truth—questions raised by hearers; questions we still don't know what to do with ourselves; questions that the Church as a whole has barely begun to wrestle with, in part because the questions themselves are yet in the process of being formulated. Perhaps as you experiment with preaching, teaching, or speaking on the topic of truth in your community, you'll be moved to write a second volume on all the messy, emerging questions still lingering. But we have to start somewhere. Just because we don't have everything worked out yet doesn't mean we can't start practicing the bits that we do. Like children learning a language, we initially engage in a lot of pointing and repeating the same words over and over again and fitting those words into established patterns, admittedly with mistakes. But soon we find that our days of Babel have given way to something resembling understanding, something that will enable us to communicate with one another. And we realize we can start experimenting with our acquired language in new ways.

One of those next experiments is to merge the vocabulary and grammar of truth with the vocabulary and grammar of religious faith. As I said in the beginning of the book, I think we sometimes try to do this prematurely, when we don't yet really know what we mean by truth. We end up with statements such as "With Jesus, we have the truth." Problematic, given that truth by definition is not any more possessable than the sky. But once we have a basic grasp of the vocabulary and grammar of truth—in essence, a familiarity with the four facets of truth we've talked about—we can begin to ponder core faith convictions at whole new levels. For instance . . .

When we say, "God is truth," do we mean God is real? Or that God is the ground out of which all of reality moves and breathes and has its being—the Reality? Or that God is the Ultimate Good? Or that God's Word is truthful about the way things really are and will be? Or that God is faithful and trustworthy? Or perhaps that everyone has a "god"—an ultimate around which they center their lives (e.g., money, security, family)—and that truth is the value that we should center our lives around? That truth should be our "god"?[1]

When Jesus said of himself, "I am the way and the truth and the life" (Jn 14:6), what did *he* mean? Was he saying that his words opened up the path to what is most real? That his preaching revealed the "deep-down truth of things"?[2] Or by drawing on the name God revealed to Moses as God's own—I AM—was Jesus identifying himself with God, who is the deepest reality that there is, the source of all reality? Or is Jesus implying that there is a profound affinity between himself and *whatever* is true, so that when one finds something true or is in a relationship that is true and clings to that truth, it leads one to Jesus?[3]

When the prologue of John's gospel names Jesus as the Word of God (Jn 1:1–18), what are we to understand? That Jesus' teaching is aligned with God's mind? Or that Jesus is the embodiment of all God revealed in the Hebrew Scriptures? Or that Jesus is the expression of God's love and fidelity in the form of a person? And what then does it mean to say that the Bible is the Word of God and that the Bible is true? From a Catholic perspective, we do not claim that it means every statement in the text is factually accurate. The Bible is not meant to be read as a scientifically historical record of events. But in what way is it nevertheless true? In the soundness of its moral judgments? In its honesty about the way the world looks from God's perspective? In its trustworthiness over the course of time, allowing generation after generation to encounter the heart of God? Is it true in ways we've not yet grasped?

In the Catholic tradition all of the above (and more!) are possibilities. In the introduction to this book, we compared truth to a multifaceted diamond. As we come to the close, we can grasp how a fuller understanding of the multiple facets of the word *truth* allows this diamond to function like a prism through which the brilliance of our faith shines forth in a wider array of colors. Christianity becomes only more beautiful and the prospects for talking about truth only more expansive. Are you ready to take on that adventure now as well?

Preaching and teaching about truth are never for the faint of heart. But truth is a central theme in our Christian faith. We *may* talk about it.

It is a source of great confusion and tension for our current hearers. We *should* talk about it.

After working your way to the end of this book, I hope you feel greater confidence that we *can* talk about it.

So only one question remains: *Will* we talk about truth?

I promise to pray for your efforts. May God grant you clarity and courage to embrace the invitation to talk about truth in your own community. I ask you to also pray for my efforts as well. May our words continue to create bridges to worlds otherwise unreachable, and do things that we could never do on our own.

THANK YOU . . .

Nothing I have ever written has caused me more angst than this book. I began with a tangled set of questions that only gradually became clearer because of the number of people who helped me talk through them. These people included my husband, Miguet, and son, Micah; a whole host of Dominicans, especially Fr. Scott Steinkerchner, Sr. Diane Kennedy, Fr. Charlie Bouchard, and Fr. Don Goergen; and many truth-loving friends, especially Carolyn Wright, Celeste Mueller, Dee Joyner, Brenda Pehle, Sue Clancy, the Rev. Canon Donna Joy, Doug Stone, and Sheila Heen. Eileen Ponder was particularly patient in reading and rereading multiple drafts while my thoughts were still half-baked. I will remember this when I fill out her canonization paperwork.

I owe a particular debt of gratitude to the Marten family and my Marten Program colleagues—Fr. Mike Connors, Karla Bellinger, Tim Matovina—at the University of Notre Dame, who made possible a semester away to finish the book. My husband told me I couldn't come home again until I was finished with the blessed thing. Fortunately, fifteen weeks and an insightful group of Preaching II students was just what I needed to wrap up the project.

PREACHING ASSESSMENT TOOL

Name of Homily and/or Name of Preacher: _____

_____

Scripture Text for the Preaching: _____

_____

EFFECTIVE PREACHING . . .

. . . has one point	How would you summarize the message of this preaching in thirty words or fewer?
. . . imitates conversational language	Was the language and tone used in this preaching the type of language and tone that might be used among friends? Were there words or ideas that you think would be too difficult for the average person in your congregation to grasp? If so, list them.

. . . *is strangely specific*	Can you point to any examples where the preaching particularly resonated with your life (e.g., in the question it was addressing, in the images or examples that were used)? Were there any particular phrases or images that struck you as you heard/read them?
. . . *emphasizes autonomy and appreciation*	Did you feel as if the preacher appreciated the struggles you face and the efforts you are making? Did the preacher respect your intelligence and freedom to make choices about your life? Can you give any examples from the preaching where you felt this?
. . . *anticipates a diversity of perspectives*	Did the preaching assume that congregants might have a diversity of perspectives on the topic at hand and treat those perspectives as charitably as possible, resisting the temptation to further an us-versus-them paradigm? Can you give any examples from the preaching where you saw this?

Twenty-four hours after reading or hearing this preaching, what is the one thing about the preaching that you suspect you will still remember? Why do you think that point will stick?

NOTES

Introduction

1. Personal Facebook conversation, December 20, 2018.

1. Truth as a Way of Seeing the World

1. Thomas Aquinas, *Summa Theologiae* 1.16.1.

2. Michael P. Lynch, *True to Life: Why Truth Matters* (Cambridge, MA: MIT Press, 2004), 10.

3. The opening of this preaching closely parallels the dilemma posed in Lynch, *True to Life*, 15. I am grateful for his unique insight into how to address the question of "seeing."

4. Francis, General Audience, November 23, 2016 https://w2.vatican.va/content/francesco/en/audiences/2016/documents/papa-francesco_20161123_udienza-generale.html.

5. Ludwig Wittgenstein, *On Certainty*, trans. G. E. M. Anscombe and G. H. von Wright (New York: Harper, 1972), 245. Quoted in Scott Steinkerchner, *Beyond Agreement: Interreligious Dialogue Amid Persistent Differences* (New York: Rowman & Littlefield, 2010), 42.

6. Anselm of Canterbury, "Truth is, indeed, in our senses, but not always; for they sometimes deceive us." Quoted by Thomas Aquinas in *Quaestiones disputatae de veritate* 1.11.

7. Rainer Maria Rilke, "Letter dated July 16, 1903," *Letters to a Young Poet*, ed. Ray Soulard (Portland, OR: Scriptor Press, 2001), 14.

8. Lynch, *True to Life*, 33.

9. For a deeper consideration of this topic, see Timothy Radcliffe, "The Wellspring of Hope," in *Sing a New Song: The Christian Vocation* (Springfield, IL: Templegate Publishers, 1999), 60: "If our century has been so marked by violence it is surely partly because it has lost confidence in our ability to attain truth together. Violence is the only resort in a culture which has no trust in the shared search for truth. Dachau, Hiroshima, Rwanda, Bosnia—these are all symbols of the collapse of a belief in the possibility of building a common human home through dialogue."

10. See especially the International Theological Commission, "Theology Today: Perspectives, Principles, and Criteria," *Origins* 41, no. 40 (March 15, 2012), 653. "Created in the image and likeness of God (Gen 1:26–27), the human person is capable, by the light of reason, of penetrating beyond appearances to the deep-down truth of things, and opens up thereby to universal reality. The common reference to truth, which is objective and universal, makes authentic dialogue possible between human persons. The human spirit is both intuitive and rational. It is intuitive in that it spontaneously grasps the first principles of reality and of thought. It is rational in that, beginning from those first principles, it progressively discovers truths previously unknown using rigorous procedures of analysis and investigation, and it organizes them in a coherent fashion. 'Science' is the highest form that rational consciousness takes. It designates a form of knowledge capable of explaining how and why things are as they are. Human reason, itself part of created reality, does not simply project on to reality in its richness and complexity a framework of intelligibility; it adapts itself to the intrinsic intelligibility of reality. In accordance with its object, that is with the particular aspect of reality that it is studying, reason applies different methods adapted to the object

itself. Rationality, therefore, is one but takes a plurality of forms, all of which are rigorous means of grasping the intelligibility of reality. Science likewise is pluriform, each science having its own specific object and method."

11. See especially Aquinas, *Summa Theologiae* 1-2.57.2.

12. Fifth Lateran Council (1516). Quoted in Robert P. Waznak, *An Introduction to the Homily* (Collegeville, MN: Liturgical Press, 1998), 8.

13. For a further exegetical introduction to the magi and especially theories about the star and its scant noting in other sources, see Raymond Brown, *The Birth of the Messiah: A Commentary on the Infancy Narratives in the Gospels of Matthew and Luke* (New York: Doubleday, 1979), 166–77.

14. Augustine of Hippo, *Confessions* 10, 54.

15. Aquinas, *Summa Theologiae* 2-2.167, A.2. For an excellent article further exploring the nature of curiosity as both a virtue and a vice, see Elias Baumgarten, "Curiosity as a Moral Virtue," *International Journal of Applied Philosophy* 15, no. 2 (Fall 2001): 169–84. Note that Aquinas does speak favorably of *studiositas* (studiousness). His use of this term perhaps more closely parallels our contemporary praise for curiosity as a virtue. See *Summa Theologiae* 2-2.166.1.

16. Marc Zvi Brettler, *How to Read the Bible* (Philadelphia: Jewish Publication Society, 2005), 44–46.

17. For more information, see "Medical Experiments," United States Holocaust Memorial Museum, https://www.ushmm.org/collections/bibliography/medical-experiments.

18. For more information, see "Tuskegee Study Timeline," Centers for Disease Control and Prevention," https://www.cdc.gov/tuskegee/timeline.htm.

2. Truth as a Way of Forming Good Judgments

1. What I present here is in simplified form. The original ladder of inference designed by Argyris has seven rungs. See Chris

Argyris, *Overcoming Organizational Defenses: Facilitating Organizational Learning* (Upper Saddle River, New Jersey: Prentice Hall, 1990). Argyris's thought was popularized by Peter Senge in *The Fifth Discipline: The Art and Practice of the Learning Organization* (New York: Doubleday, 1990). The images of the Ladder of Inference included in this chapter are used with permission, courtesy of Triad Consulting Group (triadconsultinggroup.com).

2. Aquinas, *Quaestiones disputatae de veritate*, 1.11. http://dhspriory.org/thomas/english/QDdeVer1.htm#11. Note that in this article, Thomas also quotes the twelfth-century Christian thinker Anselm of Canterbury, who states, "It seems to me that truth or falsity is not in the sense but in opinion."

3. Aquinas, *Metaphysics* 3.3: "As nobody can judge a case unless he hears the reasons on both sides, so he who has to listen to philosophy will be in a better position to pass judgment if he listens to all the arguments on both sides."

4. Douglas Stone, Bruce Patton, and Sheila Heen, *Difficult Conversations: How to Discuss What Matters Most*, 10th ann. ed. (New York: Penguin, 2010).

5. David Augsberger, *Caring Enough to Hear and Be Heard* (Ventura, CA: Regal Books, 1982), 12.

6. Aquinas, *Summa Theologiae* 2-1.94.4. Aquinas offers the example of theft—widely regarded as a wrong. He notes when something is stolen it should be returned to the rightful owner, but he then adds, "Now this is true for the majority of cases. But it may happen in a particular case that it would be injurious, and therefore unreasonable, to restore goods held in trust; for instance, if they are claimed for the purpose of fighting against one's country. And this principle will be found to fail the more, according as we descend further into detail, e.g., if one were to say that goods held in trust should be restored with such and such a guarantee, or in such and such a way; because the greater the number of conditions added, the greater the number of ways in which the principle may fail, so that it be not right to restore or not to restore." In essence,

Aquinas argues that the more particular we move in terms of context, the greater the need for prudence to figure out what would be the greatest good in this circumstance.

7. Michael Paul Gallagher, S.J., analyzes this theme as found especially in the writing and preaching of Pope John Paul II in *Clashing Symbols: An Introduction to Faith and Culture* (Mahwah, New Jersey: Paulist Press, 2003), 49-62.

8. Pius XI, *Quadragesimo Anno*, Libreria Editrice Vaticana, May 15, 1931, para. 79 http://w2.vatican.va/content/pius-xi/en/encyclicals/documents/hf_p-xi_enc_19310515_quadragesimo-anno.html. "Just as it is gravely wrong to take from individuals what they can accomplish by their own initiative and industry and give it to the community, so also it is an injustice and at the same time a grave evil and disturbance of right order to assign to a greater and higher association what lesser and subordinate organizations can do. For every social activity ought of its very nature to furnish help to the members of the body social, and never destroy and absorb them."

9. "Bubble-Hopping (Reality Part Two)," *Invisibilia*, June 8, 2017, https://www.npr.org/2017/06/08/531905309/reality-part-two. See also the follow-up to this episode, "Bonus: Catch-Up with Max Hawkins," December 22, 2017, https://www.npr.org/2017/12/22/572696073/bonus-catch-up-with-max-hawkins. Max's app is available at https://findrandomevents.com.

10. "Bonus: Catch-Up with Max Hawkins."

11. G. K. Chesterton, quoted by Bishop Robert Barron, "Looking for the Nones," YouTube video, 1:04:22, March 7, 2018, https://www.youtube.com/watch?v=tuQq3nn15ZE.

12. "Bonus: Catch-Up with Max Hawkins."

13. Aquinas, *Summa Theologiae* 2-2.70.3.2: "Good is to be presumed of everyone unless the contrary appears, provided this does not threaten injury to another."

14. For those wanting to hone their own skills in this area, I recommend Douglas Stone, Bruce Patton, and Sheila Heen, *Difficult*

Conversations: How to Discuss What Matters Most, 10th ann. ed. (New York: Penguin, 2010).

15. Joan Chittister, quoted by Teri Bays in *Joan Chittister, The Play*, act 3, accessed March 20, 2019, http://www.joanchittister. org/new/joan-chittister-play.

16. Francis, "Message of Pope Francis for the 48th World Communications Day," Libreria Editrice Vaticana, June 1, 2014, http://w2.vatican.va/content/francesco/en/messages/communications/documents/papa-francesco_20140124_messaggio-comunicazioni-sociali.html.

17. As an example of one of the seminal studies on this topic, see Peter C. Wason, "On the Failure to Eliminate Hypotheses in a Conceptual Task," *Quarterly Journal of Experimental Psychology* 12, no. 3 (1960): 129–40.

18. Andrew Solomon, "Deaf," in *Far from the Tree: Parents, Children, and the Search for Identity* (New York: Scribner, 2012), eBook.

19. Aquinas, *Metaphysics* 12.9.

3. Truth as a Way of Communicating with Others

1. The Church's teaching is rooted in Thomas Aquinas, *Summa Theologiae* 2-2.109.3.1: "Since man is a social animal, one man naturally owes another whatever is necessary for the preservation of human society. Now it would be impossible for men to live together unless they believed one another, as declaring the truth one to another."

2. For concise, meaningful commentary on the Christian understanding of the purposes of communication, see Francis, "Message of His Holiness Pope Francis for World Communications Day," Libreria Editrice Vaticana, January 24, 2018, https:// w2.vatican.va/content/francesco/en/messages/communications/ documents/papa-francesco_20180124_messaggio-comunicazioni-sociali.html.

3. Aquinas, *Summa Theologiae* 2-2.109.1. "I answer that, Truth can be taken in two ways. First, for that by reason of which a thing is said to be true, and thus truth is not a virtue, but the object or end of a virtue: because, taken in this way, truth is not a habit, which is the genus containing virtue, but a certain equality between the understanding or sign and the thing understood or signified, or again between a thing and its rule. . . . Secondly, truth may stand for that by which a person says what is true, in which sense one is said to be truthful. This truth or truthfulness must needs be a virtue, because to say what is true is a good act: and virtue is that which makes its possessor good, and renders his action good."

4. Aquinas, *Summa Theologiae* 2-2.112.1.

5. Aquinas, *Summa Theologiae* 2-2.113.1.

6. Aquinas, *Summa Theologiae* 2-2.58.1.

7. Aquinas, *Summa Theologiae* 2-2.109.3.1.

8. Aquinas, *Summa Theologiae* 2-2.23.7–8. "Now it is evident, in accordance with what has been said, that it is charity which directs the acts of all other virtues to the last end, and which, consequently, also gives the form to all other acts of virtue."

9. These questions over time have been attributed to Socrates, the Buddha, Billy Graham, and numerous others. For more information on the source of this rubric, see "If You Propose to Speak Always Ask Yourself, Is It True, Is It Necessary, Is It Kind?" Fake Buddha Quotes, accessed September 9, 2019. https://fakebuddhaquotes.com/if-you-propose-to-speak-always-ask-yourself-is-it-true-is-it-necessary-is-it-kind.

10. Aquinas, *Summa Theologiae* 2-2.110.1. Note that Aquinas draws heavily on Augustine, *De mendacio* 4.

11. Thomas Aquinas seems to have wrestled personally a great deal with this question as evidenced in *Summa Theologiae* 2-2.110.3. He gives the example of the story of the midwives found in Exodus 1. The pharaoh had ordered the Egyptian midwives to kill Hebrew baby boys as soon as they were born. When he later asked them why this wasn't happening, the midwives claimed that Hebrew

women were so strong that the babies were born before they ever
arrived on the scene. Scripture says that God rewarded these midwives. Aquinas concludes that they were rewarded not for their
lie but for their "fear of God and goodwill." In essence, you may
not need to say all you know to the pharaoh, but lying itself is
always wrong. According to Aquinas, "It is unnatural and undue
for anyone to signify by words something that is not in his mind."

12. Immanuel Kant, *Practical Philosophy*, trans. Mary Gregor
(New York: Cambridge University Press, 1996), 427: "For truthfulness is a duty that must be regarded as the basis of all duties
to be grounded on contract, the laws of which is made uncertain
and useless if even the least exception to it is admitted. To be
truthful (honest) in all declarations is therefore a sacred command
of reason prescribing unconditionally, one not to be restricted by
any conveniences."

13. As an example of a philosopher taking on this point of
view, see Michael Lynch, *True to Life: Why Truth Matters* (Cambridge, MA: MIT Press, 2004), 147–57.

14. Potential citations are too numerous to include, but key
passages to consider include Proverbs 6:16–19; Psalm 119:29;
Psalm 120:2; Proverbs 12:22; Revelation 21:8; Ephesians 4:25;
and Colossians 3:9.

15. Aquinas, *Summa Theologiae* 2-2.111.1. Aquinas refers to the
general behavior as dissimulation and describes hypocrisy as one
form of dissimulation: "It belongs to the virtue of truth to show
oneself outwardly by outward signs to be such as one is. Now
outward signs are not only words, but also deeds. Accordingly, just
as it is contrary to truth to signify by words something different
from that which is in one's mind, so also is it contrary to truth to
employ signs of deeds or things to signify the contrary of what is
in oneself, and this is what is properly denoted by dissimulation.
Consequently dissimulation is properly a lie told by the signs of
outward deeds."

16. See commentary in Ronald Rolheiser, *The Holy Longing: The Search for a Christian Spirituality* (New York: Doubleday, 1999), 227. Similarly, see Fyodor Dostoevsky, *The Brothers Karamazov*, trans. Constance Garnett (New York: Lowell Press, 2009), 48. "Above all, do not lie to yourself. A man who lies to himself and listens to his own lie comes to a point where he does not discern any truth either in himself or anywhere around him, and thus falls into disrespect towards himself and others. Not respecting anyone, he ceases to love, and having no love, he gives himself up to passions and coarse pleasures, in order to occupy and amuse himself, and in his vices reaches complete bestiality, and it all comes from lying continually to others and to himself."

17. General Assembly of the Synod of Bishops, *Instrumentum Laboris*: Young People, the Faith and Vocational Discernment," accessed January 20, 2019, http://www.synod2018.va/content/synod2018/en/fede-discernimento-vocazione/instrumentum-laboris-for-the-synod-2018--young-people--the-faith.html.

18. Francis, "Message of His Holiness Pope Francis for World Communications Day," Libreria Editrice Vaticana, January 24, 2018, sec. 1, https://w2.vatican.va/content/francesco/en/messages/communications/documents/papa-francesco_20180124_messaggio-comunicazioni-sociali.html.

19. "Message of His Holiness Pope Francis for World Communications Day," sec. 2.

20. For greater depth on the Church's teaching concerning use of social communications media, see also the *Catechism of the Catholic Church* 2493–2499.

4. Truth as a Way of Being in Relationship

1. Francis, "Pope Francis' Full Homily at the Chrism Mass," Rome Reports, March 29, 2018, https://www.romereports.com/en/2018/03/29/pope-francis-full-homily.

2. The eleventh-century Sarum Rite wedding vows—the earliest known in the English language—read: "I N. take the N. to my weddyd wyf, to have and to hold fro thys day forwarde, for better for wors, for richer for porer, in siknesse and in healthe, tyl deth us departe, yf holy Chyrche wyl it ordeyne; and thereto I plight the my trouthe."

3. For more information on trouthe-plight between friends, see Alan Bray, *The Friend* (Chicago: University of Chicago Press, 2003); and Eve Tushnet, "Beyond Religious Life and Marriage: A Look at Friendship as Vocation," *America Magazine* 216, no. 3 (February 6, 2017): https://www.americamagazine.org/faith/2017/01/24/beyond-religious-life-and-marriage-look-friendship-vocation.

4. Francis, "Pope Francis' Full Homily at the Chrism Mass."

5. William Shakespeare, *Hamlet*, 1.3.78–81. "To thine own self be true, and it must follow, as the night the day, thou canst not then be false to any man."

6. See, for example, Galatians 5:17–20; Philippians 3:3–9; Romans 7:5; and Romans 8:5–8.

7. *The Book of Alternative Services of the Anglican Church of Canada* (Toronto: Anglican Book Center, 1985) makes this point well in the liturgical introduction to "The Celebration and Blessing of a Marriage": "In marriage, husband and wife give themselves to each other, to care for each other in good times and in bad. They are linked to each other's families, and they begin a new life together in the community. It is a way of life that all should reverence, and none should lightly undertake" (541–42).

8. Terrance Klein, "Vows Are for Life," *America: The Jesuit Review*, October 1, 2015, https://www.americamagazine.org/content/good-word/vows-are-life.

9. Maria Konnikova, "The Limits of Friendship," *New Yorker*, October 7, 2014, http://www.newyorker.com/science/maria-konnikova/social-media-affect-math-dunbar-number-friendships.

10. Robin Dunbar, in Konnikova, "The Limits of Friendship."

11. Augustine of Hippo, *De doctrina Christiana*, 1.28.29.

12. Aquinas, *Summa Theologiae* 2-2.31.2.1.

13. Aquinas, *Summa Theologiae* 2-2.26.6.1.

14. Aquinas, *Summa Theologiae* 2-2.31.3.

15. Aquinas, *Summa Theologiae* 2-2.101.1.

16. "Biography," Jean Vanier Official Site, accessed March 19, 2019, https://www.jean-vanier.org/en/meet-jean/biography.

17. "Jean Vanier Official Site," Jean Vanier Official Site, accessed March 19, 2019, http://www.jean-vanier.org/en/publications/living_quotes.

18. Fyodor Dostoevsky, *The Brothers Karamazov*, trans. Constance Garnett (New York: Lowell Press, 2009), 67.

5. Truth, Next Steps

1. This notion is suggested in Albert Nolan's *Jesus Before Christianity* (Maryknoll, NY: Orbis Books, 1978), as well as John F. Haught's *What Is God?: How to Think about the Divine* (Mahwah, New Jersey: Paulist Press, 1986).

2. See especially the International Theological Commission, "Theology Today: Perspectives, Principles, and Criteria," *Origins* 41, no. 40 (March 15, 2012), 653.

3. The French philosopher and mystic Simone Weil captures this final thought well when she says, "It seems to me certain . . . that one can never wrestle enough with God if one does so out of pure regard for the truth. Christ likes us to prefer truth to him because, before being Christ, he is truth. If one turns aside from him to go toward the truth, one will not go far before falling into his arms." Weil, "The Love of God and Affliction," *Waiting for God*, trans. Emma Craufurd (New York: Harper & Row, 1973), 69.

Ann M. Garrido is associate professor of homiletics at Aquinas Institute of Theology in St. Louis, Missouri, where she previously directed the school's Doctorate of Ministry in Preaching program. Garrido has served as the Marten Faculty Fellow in Homiletics at the University of Notre Dame. She is the author of seven books, including the award-winning *Redeeming Administration* and *Redeeming Conflict*. She travels nationally and internationally helping communities talk about the topics they find toughest to talk about—conversations that always involve questions of truth.

She lives with her husband in Miami, Florida.